A DICTIONARY OF FOOD IN SPAIN

A Practical Guide to Menus, Dishes, Ingredients & Drinks Throughout

with over 2500 entries

Colin B. Lessell

In fond memory of
my dear friends, the hispanophiles
Jules & Fin Thurston,
formerly of Coín, Málaga, Spain

SAMPHIRE PRESS

Suthsaexe, England

Copyright © 2021 Dr. Colin B. Lessell

All rights reserved

© Colin B. Lessell

Other handbooks on foreign food language by the same author:

A Turkish Food Dictionary

Menu Chinese Made Easy

The Malaysian & Indonesian Menu Decoder (including Singapore & Brunei)

The Vietnamese Menu Decoder

Menu Thai Made Easy

The Cambodian Menu Guide

The Lao Food Guide & Dictionary

A Dictionary of Food in Spain

CONTENTS

Other handbooks on foreign food language
    by the same author............................... p. 3

Map of Spain... 4

NOTES ON USING THE DICTIONARY......... 6

Spanish pronunciation guide........................ 7

THE DICTIONARY...................................... 9

Map of Wine Regions of Mainland Spain.......... 117

Some useful words & phrases....................... 119

NOTES ON USING THE DICTIONARY

This user-friendly & comprehensive dictionary, **with over 2500 entries**, will enable you to identify the meaning of the food & drink terms of restaurants, bars, supermarkets & markets rapidly, yet is of a size small enough to be carried & used anywhere. It will be found helpful **throughout the whole of Spain** (including the Balearic & Canary Islands), & not just in the usual popular resorts or touristic restaurants. As far as *menus* are concerned, your main initial approach should be to look up the complete name of any dish, as given in ***Bold italics.*** Occasionally, you will find that a particular dish has alternative names, in which case you are directed from one to the other for its description,

e.g. *Arroz negro* = *Arròs negre*

Less frequently, you will need to look up selected component words. Both methods are catered for in this dictionary.

The great majority of entries are in the principal language of Spain, Castilian **Spanish**. Spanish *nouns* are either masculine or feminine, & the plural form of either is created by simply adding –**s** after a vowel, or –**es** after a consonant, e.g. **pescado-s** (fish), **caracol-es** (snail). However, for words ending in **z**, note that **z** changes to **c**, e.g. **nuez, nuec-es** (walnut). Whilst most nouns are entered in their singular form (without –**s** or –**es** at the end), where appropriate, some nouns are given in the plural.

Adjectives have endings which agree with the nouns they qualify, according to gender & number. Given separately, these are mainly in the masculine singular form followed by the feminine singular version, e.g. **blanco/blanca** (white). The plural forms can be simply deduced by adding –**s**, e.g. **blanco-s/blanca-s**, or –**es** after a consonant, e.g. **azul-es** (blue).

Spain, however, does have three other major languages, each with its own grammar & vocabulary. In consequence, there are a few entries given in these. The following are the abbreviations used in this dictionary to indicate the languages concerned:

Catalan : *Ctn*   ***Basque*** : *Bsq*   ***Galician*** : *Gal*

© Colin B. Lessell

As for the pronunciation of **Spanish**, here is a basic guide:

a	as **a** in f**a**ther
b	as **b** in **b**eat
c	before **e** or **i** : like **s** in **s**ip, or **th** in **th**ing (regional variation); before **a**, **o**, **u** or a **consonant** : like **k** in **k**ing
ch	as **ch** in **ch**air
d	as **d** in **d**ate; but between vowels or at the ends of a words more like **th** in **th**ough
e	like **a** in c**a**ve
f	as **f** in **f**lame
g	before **e** or **i** : like **h** in **h**ard; otherwise : as **g** in **g**oat
h	silent, even as first letter of a word (except in **ch**, *see above*)
i	like **ee** as in s**ee**
j	like **h** in **h**ard, but more in the throat
k	like **ck** as in ba**ck**
l	as **l** in **l**ack
ll	like **y** in **y**es (in some regions, like L+Y, as in **mi-LLI-on**)
m	as **m** in **m**at
n	as **n** in **n**ame
ñ	like **ny** in ca**ny**on
o	as **o** in p**o**t
p	as **p** in **p**ig
q	like **k** in **k**ite
r	**r** rolled on the tip of the tongue
rr	trilled **r** (difficult for many; rolled **r** will suffice)
s	as **s** in **s**ap
t	as **t** in **t**ug
u	as **u** in fl**u**te
v	like **b** in **b**ig
w	as **w** in **w**indow
x	as **x** in mi**x**
y	as **y** in **y**es
z	like **th** in **th**ing

Rules of stress: *If a word ends in* **-s**, **-n** *or a* **vowel**, *then the* <u>*stress*</u> *is usually on its* <u>*last but one*</u> *syllable (**80%** of words); otherwise, on its* <u>*last*</u> *syllable. Where this rule is broken, the stressed syllable is given an* <u>*accent mark*</u>, *e.g.* **azúcar.** *The accent mark is sometimes used according to other rules, but just remember that it always indicates the syllable where the stress should be applied.*

A Dictionary of Food in Spain

© Colin B. Lessell

A DICTIONARY OF FOOD IN SPAIN

When searching for the names of dishes given in menus, you should note that the following four terms of connection are occasionally substituted for each other, with little alteration in meaning:

        a la (or **al**)   *with, in the manner of*
        de (or **del**)   *of*
        con   *with*
        en   *in*

A Dictionary of Food in Spain

A

a la (a lo) 1. in the manner of 2. with

abadejo pollack (fish)
Abajá de Algeciras Algeciras style mixed fish stew
abichón 1. sand smelt (fish) 2. Mediterranean sand smelt
abierto open (shop sign)
Abona red & white wine region in southern Tenerife, Canaries
abuela Granny's style

Acehúche, queso de Extremaduran raw goat's milk cheese
aceite oil
    aceite de girasol sunflower oil
    aceite de oliva olive oil
    aceite de oliva virgen extra extra virgin olive oil
aceitunas olives
    aceitunas deshuesadas pitted olives
    aceitunas negras black olives
    aceitunas verdes green olives
~*Aceitunas con aliño de tomillo* olives marinated with thyme
acelga chard (Swiss chard)
~*Acelgas a la catalana* Catalan style chard with bacon, potatoes, raisins, pine nuts & garlic
~*Acelgas a la malagueña* Málaga style fried chard with raisins & garlic
~*Acelgas fritas* fried chard stalks
achicoría chicory

adobado[1] pickled pork
adobado[2]**/adobada** 1. marinated 2. pickled
adobo marinade
    en **adobo** 1. marinated 2. in sour sauce
Adoquines ('Paving-stones') Aragonese sweets (candies)

A Dictionary of Food in Spain

Afuega'l pitu (Asturian: 'Strangle the chicken') Asturian unpasteurized cow's milk cheese

agrio/agria sour
agua water
    agua con gas fizzy (carbonated) water
    agua de grifo tap water
    agua de manantial spring water
    agua sin gas still (uncarbonated) water
aguacate avocado
    ~Aguacate con gambas prawn (shrimp) & avocado cocktail
aguardiente distilled spirit
    aguardiente de anís aniseed brandy
    aguardiente de orujo clear grape brandy
aguja 1. gar-fish 2. beef chuck 3. pork blade bone
agulla *Ctn* gar-fish
agullat *Ctn* spur dog (fish)

ahumado/ahumada smoked

Airén white wine grape

ajada gallega Galician style piquant sauce for seafood or salad
ajiaceite = **allioli** (see under **all**)
ajillo 1. chopped garlic 2. garlic sauce
    al **ajillo** 1. with garlic 2. with garlic sauce.
ajo garlic
    ajo en polvo garlic powder
    ajo morado purple garlic
    al **ajo arriero (ajoarriero)** muleteer's style with garlic
~Ajo blanco = *Ajoblanco*
~Ajo de espárragos ('Asparagus-garlic') asparagus with garlic
~Ajo de harina = *Ajo harina*
~Ajo de la mano ('Garlic of the hand') Jaén style garlic & potato mash with paprika & cumin
~Ajo harina ('Garlic flour') Jaén style salt cod with potatoes, garlic & tomato-based sauce
ajoaceite = **allioli** (see under **all**)

Ajoblanco white garlic & almond soup, sometimes served with added grapes or melon slices
~*Ajoblanco con melón* white garlic & almond soup with melon slices
~*Ajoblanco con uvas* white garlic & almond soup with grapes
~*Ajoblanco extremeño* Extremaduran garlic, egg yolk & vegetable soup, without almonds
Ajoharina = *Ajo harina*
ajonjolí sesame seed
Ajopollo = *Cazuela de papas a la abuela*

al 1. in the manner of 2. with
alacha round sardinella (fish)
aladroc *Ctn* young anchovy (i.e. 'fry')
    aladroc fregit *Ctn* Valencian fried anchovy fry
Alajú honey & almond nougat
alatxa *Ctn* round sardinella (fish)
albacora longfin tuna
albahaca basil
albaricoques apricots
Albariño popular Galician grape variety yielding white wines
alberginies *Ctn* aubergines (eggplants)
~*Alberginies farcides* *Ctn* stuffed aubergines (eggplants)
Albillio white wine grape
Albóndigas 1. meatballs 2. fish-balls
~*Albóndigas caseras* homemade meatballs in sauce
~*Albóndigas de bacalao* salt cod fish-balls
~*Albóndigas de cerdo* pork meatballs
~*Albóndigas de ternera* beef meatballs
Alboronía Jewish-Muslim style ratatouille
albure dace (river fish)
alcachofas artichokes
~*Alcachofas al la cordobesa* Córdoba style artichoke & potato casserole
~*Alcachofas al limón* artichokes with lemon sauce
~*Alcachofas aliñadas* marinated artichokes
~*Alcachofas con arroz* green artichoke paella
~*Alcachofas con mayonesa* artichokes with mayonnaise
~*Alcachofas rebozadas* deep-fried battered artichokes

~*Alcachofas rellenos* artichokes stuffed with ground (minced) meat (pork or beef) & chopped ham
~*Alcachofas salteadas con jamon* sautéed artichokes with ham
alcaparras capers
alcaravea caraway seed
alcauciles artichokes
~*Alcauciles rellenos* Cádiz style artichokes stuffed with cheese, egg & breadcrumbs
alergia allergy
    tengo **alergia a...** I have an allergy to...
aleta beef flank steak
    aleta de ternera breast of veal
~*Aleta de ternera rellena* stuffed veal roll
Alfajores Andalusian Christmas pastry dessert, made from honey, nuts, sugar & flour
alfalfa alfalfa
alicantino/alicantina Alicante style
aligote Spanish bream (fish)
aliñado/aliñada 1. marinated 2. seasoned
aliño 1. marinade 2. sauce 3. dressing
alioli (Spanish) = **allioli** *Ctn* (see under **all**)
alita wing
    alitas de pollo chicken wings
~*Alitas de pollo fritas* fried chicken wings
~*Alitas fritas* fried chicken wings
alitán large-spotted dogfish (huss)
Áliva, queso de Cantabrian cow's milk cheese with an aroma of smoked beef
all *Ctn* garlic
    all i oli *Ctn* = **allioli** (below)
    allioli *Ctn* garlic & olive oil mayonnaise
~*All i pebre* *Ctn* Valencian area dish of peppers, garlic, potatoes & eels
almeja clam
    almeja babosa slimy clam
    almeja fina carpet-shell
    almeja japónica Japanese clam
    almejas limpias de arena clams cleaned of sand
~*Almejas a la crema* clams with cream

~*Almejas a la marinera* sailor's style clams
~*Almejas con alubias blancas* clams with white beans
~*Almejas con arroz* clams with rice
almejón brillante smooth Venus (bivalve mollusc)
Almendrados ground almond, cinnamon & egg white biscuits (cookies)
almendras almonds
    almendras de mar dog-cockles (bivalve molluscs)
    almendras tostadas toasted almonds
~*Almendras garapiñadas* sugar-coated (candied) almonds
almeriense Almería style
almíbar syrup
Almogrote Canarian spread for toast, made from cheese, peppers, garlic & olive oil
almuerzo lunch (midday meal)
alondra lark
alubias beans
    alubias blancas 1. butter beans (lima beans) 2. white beans in general (restaurant term)
    alubias rojas red kidney beans
~*Alubias cocidas* baked beans
~*Alubias con manitas de cerdo* beans with pig's trotters

Amadí Valencian festive cake with pumpkin, almonds, sugar & lemon zest.
Amanida *Ctn* Catalan salad
amargo/amarga bitter
Amarguillos dessert pastries with almonds, eggs & sugar
amarillo/amarilla yellow
    en **amarillo** in saffron sauce
amasuela (*plural* **amasueles**) clam (Asturia)
amb *Ctn* with
ameixas *Gal* clams
~*Ameixas á mariñeira* *Gal* = *Almejas a la marinera*
Amoados Galician oatmeal biscuits (cookies)
amontillado medium-dry sherry
amploia *Ctn* sprat (fish)

anacardos cashew nuts

ancas de rana frogs' legs
~Ancas de rana fritas fried frogs' legs
ancho/ancha wide
anchoa anchovy
~Anchoas en salsa amarilla Basque anchovies in yellow sauce
andaluz/andaluza Andalusian style
Andrajos ('Rags') Jaén style stew of vegetables & rag-shaped pasta with rabbit, hare or cod
androlla Galician pork sausage
añejo/ añeja 1. aged 2. well cured
anfós *Ctn* grouper (fish)
angelote monkfish (angel-fish)
anguila eel
~Anguila al all i pebre *Ctn* Valencian eel stew with garlic & paprika
~Anguilas con judías eels stewed with beans
angulas baby eels
~Angulas en cazuela baby eels with garlic
anis aniseed
anjova bluefish
añojo yearling
antequerano/antequerana Antiquera (Málaga) style
antigua old-fashioned
    al **antigua** in the old-fashioned manner
anxova *Ctn* anchovy

apio celery

aragonés/aragonesa Aragonese style
araña 1, greater weever (fish) 2. spotted weever
arándanos 1. blueberries 2. cranberries
aranya *Ctn* types of weever (fish):
    aranya blanca *Ctn* greater weever
    aranya de cap negre *Ctn* starry weever
    aranya fragata *Ctn* spotted weever
arbitán Spasnish ling (fish)
arcas de Noé Noah's arks (bivalve molluscs)
ardaurgozatza *Bsq* Basque lemonade
arena sand

arenque herring (fish)
arete red gurnard (fish)
armado armed gurnard (fish)
armat *Ctn* armed gurnard (fish)
arrain (*plural* **arrainak**) *Bsq* fish (any)
arriero muleteer style
arrop *Ctn* grape must syrup
~*Arrop i tallaetes* *Ctn* Valencian dessert of grape must syrup & slices of pumpkin (or of other fruit)
arrope grape must syrup
~*Arrope con boniatos* sweet potatoes candied in arrope
arròs *Ctn* rice (see also dishes under **arroz**)
~*Arròs a banda* *Ctn* Valencian style rice cooked in fish stock
~*Arròs a la mandra* *Ctn* = ***Paella parellada***
~*Arròs al forn* *Ctn* Valencian baked rice with sausage, chickpeas, potatoes & stew leftovers
~*Arròs amb conill i cargols* *Ctn* rice with rabbit & snails
~*Arròs amb crosta* *Ctn* Alicante style rice with various meats (including leftovers), sausage & chickpeas, covered with egg to provide the 'crust'
~*Arròs amb perdiu* *Ctn* rice with partridge
~*Arròs de la terra* *Ctn* Menorcan rice with sausage
~*Arròs de peix* *Ctn* Balearic rice cooked in fish broth, with fish
~*Arròs negre* *Ctn* ('Black rice') rice with squid ink, squid & prawns (shrimp), often eaten with **allioli** (see under **all**)
~*Arròs negre amb all i oli* *Ctn* = *Arròs negre* (with **allioli**)
arroz rice (see also dishes under **arròs**)
    arroz bomba most popular short grain rice for **paella** (see)
    arroz de grano corto short round grain rice (**paella** rice)
    arroz de grano largo long grain rice
    arroz integral brown rice
    arroz redondo = **arroz de grano corto** (above)
~*Arroz a la alicantina* Alicante style rice with artichokes, fish & green peppers (capsicums)
~*Arroz a la cubana* Canary Islands' Cuban style rice with fried egg, fried banana & tomato sauce
~*Arroz a la marinera* sailor's style rice with mixed seafood
~*Arroz a la peixator* fishmonger's style rice with crayfish, sole & gurnard

~*Arroz a la quintería* farmhouse style rice with fish & greens
~*Arroz a la zamorana* Zamora style rice with pig's trotter & ear
~*Arroz abanda* = *Arròs a banda*
~*Arroz al caldero* Murcian creamy rice cooked with fish stock & dried red **ñora** peppers in a deep cauldron-like pan
~*Arroz al cazador* hunter's style rice with rabbit
~*Arroz brut* ('Dirty rice') Mallorcan rice, meat & vegetables cooked in meat broth
~*Arroz caldoso* soupy rice with chicken, vegetables or seafood
~*Arroz con bogavante* rice with lobster
~*Arroz con borrajas y almejas* Aragonese rice with borage & clams
~*Arroz con conejo y caracoles* = *Arròs amb conill i cargols*
~*Arroz con gambas* rice with prawns (shrimp)
~*Arroz con huevo* fried egg on rice
~*Arroz con leche* creamy rice pudding
~*Arroz con liebre* rice with hare
~*Arroz con perdiz* = *Arròs amb perdiu*
~*Arroz con pollo* chicken with rice
~*Arroz del cazador* = *Arroz al cazador*
~*Arroz en perdiu* ('Rice on partridge') Valencian *meatless* vegetable & chickpea rice dish with a head of garlic as a mock partridge
~*Arroz marinero* = *Arroz a la marinera*
~*Arroz negro* = *Arròs negre*
~*Arroz parellada* = *Paella parellada*
~*Arroz rossejat* Valencian style rice, meat & sausage casserole
arrugado/arrugada 1. wrinkled 2. crumpled
arveja pea (Canaries)
Arzúa-Ulloa, queso Galician cow's milk (raw or pasteurized) soft cheese

asadillo roast
~*Asadillo de la huerta* flame-roasted garden vegetables
~*Asadillo manchego* cold La Mancha dish of roasted red peppers with tomatoes, often topped with boiled egg
asado/asada 1. roasted 2. roast
~*Asado de cerdo a la catalana* Catalan style roast pork
~*Asado de hígados de bonito* Basque roast bonito (fish) livers

~*Asado de mújol* roast grey mullet
asador restaurant specializing in grills or rotisseries
asar to roast
    para **asar** for roasting
ase *Ctn* armed gurnard (fish)
asturiano/asturiana Asturian style
Atascaburros ('Donkeys stick in the mire') thick La Mancha mashed potato, with garlic, cod, egg & nuts

atún bluefin tuna (tunny)
    atún en aceite girasol canned tunny in sunflower oil
    atún en aceite vegetal canned tunny in vegetable oil
~*Atún a la mahonesa* Balearic tuna (tunny) and mayonnaise
~*Atún con tomate* fresh tuna (tunny) baked in tomato sauce
~*Atún encebollada a la malagueña* Málaga style tuna (tunny) smothered in onions

ave 1. fowl 2. bird
    aves poultry
avellanas hazelnuts
avena oats
aves see **ave**

azafrán saffron
azahar orange blossom
azúcar sugar
    azúcar moreno brown sugar
    azúcar tamizado icing sugar

A Dictionary of Food in Spain

B

babilla beef top rump (thick flank)
baboso blenny (fish)
bacaladilla blue whiting (fish)
bacalao 1. salted dried cod 2. fresh cod
~*Bacalao a la manchega* La Mancha style salt cod cooked with potatoes & topped with eggs, popular in Castilian-La Mancha Holy Week
~*Bacalao a la vizcaína* Biscay style salt cod with dried red peppers (*not* chilies) & tomatoes
~*Bacalao al pil-pil* Basque style sizzling salt cod with garlic & chili (see **pil-pil**)
~*Bacalao al ajo arriero* muleteer's style salt cod with garlic, chili, paprika & tomato sauce
~*Bacalao con patatas* Cádiz style layered salt cod & potatoes with olives & sweet peppers (capsicums)
~*Bacalao con romescoi* salt cod with **romesco** (see) sauce
bacallà *Ctn* = **bacalao**
bacon bacon
    bacon ahumado smoked bacon
bacoreta little tunny (fish)
baila 1. spotted sea bass (fish) 2. European sea bass
bajo/baja low
    bajo en grasa low in fat
bakailao *Bsq* = **bacalao**
baldufa *Ctn* top-shell (sea snail)
Banderillas cold *Tapas* (see) made from small food items pickled in vinegar & skewered together (e.g. onions, peppers, olives)
bar bar, serving just drinks or drinks & *Tapas* (see) or *Pinchos* (see)
baratxuri *Bsq* garlic
~*Baratxuri zopa* *Bsq* garlic soup
barbacao barbecue
    a la **barbacao** barbecued

barbo barbel (river fish)
barra baguette (supermarket type)
    barra de pan baguette (from local bakery)
    barra integral wholemeal baguette
batata sweeet potato
batido milkshake
Bauma carrat goat's milk cheese from Borredà, Catalonia

bebidas drinks (in general)
becada woodcock
beicon bacon
bejel tub gurnard (fish)
Benabarre, queso de mild pasteurized Aragonese goat's cheese
berberechos cockles (bivalve molluscs)
berenjena aubergine (eggplant)
~*Berenjenas a la catalana* Catalan style aubergines with ground hazelnuts or walnuts, & tomatoes
~*Berenjenas a la morisca* Moorish style aubergines, roasted, cooled & diced, with garlic, lemon juice, chili & cumin
~*Berenjenas al horno* baked aubergines with cheese
~*Berenjenas con miel* Córdoba style fried aubergine slices, served with honey
~*Berenjenas fritas* fried floured aubergine slices
~*Berenjenas rellenas a la mallorquina* Mallorcan style aubergines stuffed with ham & minced (ground) meat
berro watercress
berza cabbage
~*Berza de acelga* Andalusian peasant stew of pork, paprika, nutmeg, marjoram, haricot beans, chard or spinach, chickpeas, lard & **chorizo** (see) sausage
besuc *Ctn* Spanish bream (fish)
besugo red bream (fish)
~*Besugo a la madrileña* Madrid style baked red bream with garlic, parsley & breadcrumbs
~*Besugo asado a la donostiarra* San Sebastian style grilled (broiled) red bream with garlic, chili & lemon juice
~*Besugo con almendras a la castellana* Castilian style baked red bream with almonds

Bica Galician sponge cake
bicarbonato sódico baking soda
bien well
    bien cocido well cooked
    bien hecho well-done (steak)
Bienmesabe ('It tastes good to me') dessert made from honey, egg yolk & ground almonds, popular in Canary Islands
Bierzo northwestern Castilian-Leonese red & white wine region
bilbaíno/bilbaína Bilbao style
bis *Ctn* chub mackerel
bisbe *Ctn* ('bishop') Catalan black (blood) pudding
bisso *Ctn* chub mackerel (fish)
bistek beef steak
Bitokes fried minced (ground) beef or veal patties
Bizcocho de aceite sponge cake
~*Bizcochos borrachos* little cakes soaked in wine

blanco/blanca white

Bobal red grape producing full-bodied wines
boca mouth
~*Bocas de la isla* Andalusian crab claws
Bocadillo sandwich, usually in bread roll or baguette
~*Bocadillo de calamares* baguette stuffed with fried battered squid rings
~*Bocadillo de carne* general term for a meat sandwich
~*Bocadillo de chistorra* sandwich of **chistorra** (see) sausage
~*Bocadillo de lomo* pork tenderloin sandwich
~*Bocadillo de pollo* chicken sandwich
~*Bocadillo de queso* cheese sandwich
~*Bocadillo de sardinas* canned sardine sandwich
~*Bocadillo serranito* bread roll filled with serrano ham, fried pork tenderloin, fried green pepper slices & tomato
bocareu anchovy
Bocata = Bocadillo
bodega 1. winery 2. wine cellar 3. bar 4. wine cellar & bar
bodiao ballan wrasse (fish)
boga bogue (fish)

bogavante lobster
~*Bogavante a la gallega* Galician style lobster with garlic, tomato & white wine (lobster liver & roe in sauce)
bola ball
Bola, queso de Edam cow's milk cheese
boletos boletus mushrooms
boliches de Embún Aragonese type of bean (several colours)
~*Boliches de Embún guisados a la antigua* Aragonese beans gently stewed in the old way with garlic, carrot & leek
Bolla de chicharrones sweet pork rind cake
Bollería pastries (in general)
Bollit Valencian vegetable stew, often a side-dish for dinner
bollo 1. bread roll 2. bun
~*Bollo de clavonia* = *bollo maimón* (below)
~*Bollo de hornazo* sweet & dry bread, decorated with hard-boiled eggs
~*Bollo maimón* type of celebratory sponge cake from Salamanca, Zamora & León
~*Bollos preñados* ('Pregnant buns') baked **chorizo** (see) & ham buns
bomba = **arroz bomba**
boniato sweet potato
bonito Atlantic bonito (fish)
~*Bonito a la bilbaína* Bilbao style starter with cold cooked bonito, eggs, onions & parsley, & served with mayonnaise
bonitol *Ctn* Atlantic bonito (fish)
boquerones 1. fresh anchovies
2. abbreviation for *Boquerones en vinagre* (below)
~*Boquerones a la malagueña* Málaga style deep-fried 'fan' of five dusted anchovies held together at their tails
~*Boquerones al nutural* = *Boquerónes en vinagre*
~*Boquerones en escabeche* = *Boquerónes en vinagre*
~*Boquerones en vinagre* fresh anchovy fillets marinated in vinegar, olive oil, parsley & garlic, a popular *Tapa* (see)
~*Boquerones rebozados* fried battered anchovies
borracho[1] grey gurnard (fish)
borracho[2]/borracha 1. soused in wine or liqueur 2. drunken
~*Borrachos* sponge cakes drizzled in sherry or Málaga wine

Borrachuelos fried donuts made with flour, aniseed, sesame seed & wine
borrajas borage
bot *Ctn* trigger-fish
botella bottle
    media **botella** half-bottle
    una **botella** *de…* a bottle of…
botellín small bottle, especially of beer (20cl =200ml)
Botelo *Gal* = ***Botillo***
botifarra *Ctn* Catalan sausage, with many varieties
    botifarra negra/negret sausage containing pig's blood
~***Botifarra amb mongetes*** *Ctn* Catalan sausage with beans
Botillo Leonese meat-stuffed pork intestine (caecum/cecum)
bovino cattle meat (in general)

brasa ember
    a la **brasa** charcoal-grilled (charcoal-broiled)
brazo arm
~***Brazo de gitano*** ('Gypsy's arm') Swiss roll
~***Brazo de gitano de patatas*** potato roll with minced (ground) meat stuffing
brazuelo beef shin
breca pandora (fish)
brecól broccoli
breva early fig
Brez, queso de Cantabrian smoked or unsmoked cow's milk cheese
brocheta 1. skewer 2. kebab
~***Brocheta de pez espada*** swordfish kebab
broculi broccoli
brote beansprout
brótola greater forkbeard (fish)
    brótola de roca forkbeard
brut dry sparkling wine (see **cava**)

buche Extremaduran meat-stuffed intestine (caecum/cecum)
Budín 1. pudding (sweet) 2. pie (savoury)
buey 1. ox 2. beef from older beast
    buey del mar large edible crab

Bulavesa fish stew (Spanish version of French Bouillabaisse)
bull negre *Ctn* Catalan black (blood) pudding
Buñuelo 1. fritter 2. puff
~***Buñuelos de bacalao*** salt cod fritters
~***Buñuelos de batata*** sweet potato fritters
~***Buñuelos de higo*** fig fritters
~***Buñuelos de queso*** cheese puffs
~***Buñuelos de viento*** ('Puffs of wind') Spanish profiteroles
Bunyol *Ctn* = ***Buñuelo***
Burgos, queso de fresh soft cheese from Castille-León made from raw or pasteurized cow's & sheep's milk
búsano whelk (single-shell mollusc)
Butiellu = ***Botillo***
butifarra = **botifarra**

C

caballa Atlantic mackerel (fish)
~Caballa al horno baked mackerel
~Caballa rellena mackerel stuffed with minced (ground) mixed fish
cabañil muleteer's style
cabeçuda *Ctn* big-scale sand smelt (fish)
cabello hair
    cabello de angel ('angel's hair') jam from **cidra** (see), & used as a filling for pies, cakes or pastries
cabeza 1. head 2. pig's head
    cabeza de ajo head of garlic
cabra 1. goat 2. blue-mouth (fish) 3. spider crab *Ctn*
    cabra de altura blue-mouth (fish)
Cabra, queso de goat's cheese
cabracho red scorpion fish
~Cabracho en salsa verde red scorpion fish in green sauce (made from leeks & parsley) with potatoes
Cabrales, queso de Asturian blue cheese from unpasteurized cow's milk, or a blend of cow's with goat's or sheep's
cabrilla comber (fish)
cabrit *Ctn* kid (baby goat)
~Cabrit o lechona es forn *Ctn* Menorcan roasted kid or piglet
cabrito kid (baby goat)
~Cabrito asado roast kid (goat)
cacahuetes peanuts
cacerola 1. casserole 2. saucepan
Cachelada Leonese potatoes with ham & **chorizo** (see)
Cachelos Galician style boiled potatoes
Cachopo two Asturian style veal (or beef), ham & cheese schnitzels
cachón cuttlefish
~Cachón en su tinta Cantabrian cuttlefish cooked in its own ink
cachorreña bitter orange (Seville orange)

Cachuela Extremaduran fatty seasoned pork liver pâté
cadera 1. beef silverside (outside or bottom round)
2. beef rump
café coffee (see also **carajillo, cortado, largo**)
    café americano regular black coffee
    café bombón espresso coffee with condensed milk
    café con gotas coffee with a little liquor of choice
    café con leche coffee with milk
    café descafeinado decaffeinated coffee
    café espresso small strong shot of coffee
    café fuerte strong white coffee
    café irlandesa Irish coffee
    café solo small strong coffee
cafetería basic cheap restaurant serving one plate meals, often with bread & a drink included; also coffee, tea & cakes
cailón porbeagle shark
calabacín 1. courgette (zucchini) 2. small marrow
~*Calabacines al horno* baked courgettes
~*Calabacines rellenos* stuffed courgettes
calabaza 1. pumpkin 2. squash (vegetable)
~*Calabaza frita* fried pumpkin
~*Calabaza guisada* stewed pumpkin
calamar squid
~*Calamares a la romana* deep-fried battered squid rings
~*Calamares en su tinta* squid cooked in its own ink
~*Calamares rellenos* stuffed squid
~*Calamares rellenos con jamón* braised squid stuffed with ham
calçot *Ctn* type of spring onion (scallion)
Calçotada de Valls *Ctn* Catalan style grilled (broiled) spring onions (scallions)
Caldeirada *Gal* Galician fish stew
~*Caldeirada da raia* *Gal* Galician fish stew with skate wings (especially eaten at the *Fiesta da Raia*, Portonovo)
~*Caldeirada de raya* = *Caldeirada da raia*
Caldera *Ctn* stew
~*Caldera de cigalas* Menorcan langoustine stew
~*Caldera de llagosta* Menorcan lobster stew
~*Caldera de mero* Menorcan grouper stew

Caldereta stew
~*Caldereta asturiana* Asturian style fish & shellfish stew
~*Caldereta de chivo* goat stew
~*Caldereta de cordero* lamb stew
~*Caldereta de langosta* Menorcan spiny lobster cooked in tomato, onion & garlic sauce
~*Calderata extremeña* Extremaduran kid (goat) garlicky stew
~*Calderata manchega* La Mancha style lamb stew
caldero 1. cauldron 2. deep cauldron-like pan
    al **caldero** cooked in either of the above
Caldillo 1. soup 2. = *Cachuela* (Extremadura)
~*Caldillo de perro* ('Dog soup') Cádiz style fish (hake) soup with the juice of bitter oranges (*no* dog meat here!)
caldito bouillon cube
Caldo 1. soup 2. consommé 3. broth 4. stock 5. wine
    caldo de carne beef stock
    caldo de pollo chicken stock
    caldo de verduras vegetable stock
    los **caldos de La Rioja** the wines of the Rioja region
~*Caldo de papas* potato soup
~*Caldo de pescado* fish soup
~*Caldo de pimentón* red pepper soup
~*Caldo gallego* Galician style soup with beans, beef & greens
caldoso/caldosa soupy
Calentitos fried dough snack (Seville)
~*Calentitos de papas* = *Churros*
~*Calentitos de Rueda* = *Calientes*
caliente 1. hot 2. warm
~*Calientes* thicker Sevillian version of *Churros* (see)
calimocho Basque drink of red wine mixed with cola
callos tripe
~*Callos a la andaluza* = *Menudo gitano*
~*Callos a la madrileña* Madrid style tripe with calf's foot
~*Callos con manos de cerdo* tripe with pig's feet
camarera waitress
camarero waiter
camarón small common prawn (shrimp)
Camerano, queso goat's milk cheese from
    Sierra de Cameros, La Rioja

caña small cylindrical glass of draught beer (about 200ml)
    Caña de cabra Murcian soft goat's milk cheese log
    Caña de oveja Murcian soft ewe's milk cheese log
cañadillas murex (single-shell mollusc)
canario/canaria Canarian style
canela cinnamon
    canela en rama cinnamon stick
canelones cannelloni
~*Canelones a la catalana* Catalan style festive dish of cannelloni filled with chicken, chicken livers, pork or veal, & lamb's brains
cangrejo crab
    cangrejo de mar shore crab (two species)
    cangrejo de río crayfish
    cangrejo moruno shore crab (two more species)
~*Cangrejos de rio al jerez* crayfish with sherry
~*Cangrejos de rio con tomate* crayfish with tomato
canónigos lamb's lettuce (Valerianella locusta)
cantelo Asturian bread ring for weddings
càntera *Ctn* black bream (fish)
cap *Ctn* 1. head 2. cap
    cap de costella de porc *Ctn* pork rib head
    cap de costella de xai *Ctn* lamb rib head
    cap roig *Ctn* red scorpion fish, popular in Mallorca
~*Cap roig con salsa de almendras* red scorpion fish in almond sauce
caparrón type of red kidney bean
~*Caparrones* La Rioja style stew of red beans & **chorizo** (see)
capellán poor cod
capitán flathead grey mullet (fish)
capitón 1. flathead grey mullet (fish) 2. thin-lip grey mullet 3. white mullet 4. bluespot mullet
caqui persimmon
carabinero large common prawn (shrimp)
caracolas sea snails
caracoles snails
    caracoles grises top-shells (sea snails)
~*Caracoles a la levantina* Levantine style snails with cumin & chili

~*Caracoles a la patarrallada* charcoal grilled (broiled) snails served with **allioli** (see under **all**)
caragols *Ctn* = **cargols**
carajillo = **café con gotas**
caramel picarel
caramujos top-shells (sea snails)
carbonera type of wild mushroom
carbonero saithe (coalfish, coley)
Carcamusas Toledo style pork 'chili con carne'
cardaire *Ctn* bottlenose skate (fish)
cardamomos cardamoms
cardo cardoon (artichoke thistle)
~*Cardos en salsa de almendras* cardoons in almond sauce
~*Cardos fritos* fried battered cardoons
cargols *Ctn* snails
~*Cargols a la llauna* *Ctn* snails cooked in a metal pan under a grill (broiler) or in an oven
Cariñeña red wine grape
carne meat
    carne de membrillo = **dulce de membrillo**
    carne picada minced (ground) meat
~*Carne asada a la sevillana* Sevillian style beef pot roast
~*Carne fiesta* ('Party meat') Canarian festive dish of marinated fried meat, usually pork
~*Carne mechada* slowly cooked tender beef *Tapa* (see)
~*Carne ó caldeiro* *Gal* Galician beef & potatoes
carnero mutton
carnicería butcher's shop
carpa carp
Carquinyolis *Ctn* almond biscuits (cookies)
carrillada 1. pig's cheek 2. ox cheek
~*Carrillada de cerdo* Sevillian style gently stewed pig's cheek
~*Carrillada ibérico* = *Carrillada de cerdo* (above)
carrillera = **carillada**
la **carta** menu
cártamo safflower
carxofes *Ctn* artichokes
Casadielles Galician & Asturian walnut pastry rolls

cascara nut shell
   sin **cascara** without shell
casero/casera[1] homemade
   La **Casera**[2] Spanish carbonated (fizzy) lemonade brand
Casín, queso Asturian hard or semi-hard cow's milk cheese
Casquetes Ctn = *Pastissets*
cassola *Ctn* casserole
castañas chestnuts
~*Castañas con leche* chestnuts in milk dessert
castanyola *Ctn* Ray's bream (fish)
castellano/castellana Castilian style
catalán/catalana Catalan style
Catània (plural *Catànies*) *Ctn* almonds coated with chocolate
cateto 1. rustic 2. country style
   pan **cateto** rustic bread
cava Spanish sparkling white & pink wines produced by the champagne method, of which there are seven basic types from very dry to sweet: brut nature (no added sugar), extra brut, brut, extra seco, seco, semi-seco, dulce
cavach *Ctn* bottlenose skate (fish)
cayena 1. chili pepper 2. cayenne pepper
cazador hunter's style
cazadora huntress' style
cazón tope shark
~*Cazón en adobo* fried marinated tope (shark) *Tapa* (see)
Cazuela casserole
~*Cazuela a la catalana* Catalan style minced (ground) beef & vegetables, fried & braised; with **botifarra** (see) garnish
~*Cazuela de chivo* kid (goat) casserole
~*Cazuela de espinacas con huevos a la granadina* Granada style spinach & eggs
~*Cazuela de espinacas y mejillones* mussels & spinach casserole
~*Cazuela de fideos* seafood spaghetti casserole
~*Cazuela de habas a la granadina* Granada style broad bean & artichoke casserole
~*Cazuela de judías verdes con chorizo* Green beans & **chorizo** (see) sausage casserole

~*Cazuela de lentejas* lentil casserole with spicy pork link or red sausage
~*Cazuela de papas a la abuela* Granny's potato cassserole with almonds & garlic, sometimes with fish or shellfish

cebada[1] barley
cebado/cebada[2] fattened (as with livestock)
cebolla onion
    cebolla tierna spring onion (scallion)
~*Cebollas guisadas* braised tiny onions
cebollinos chives
Cebreiro, queixo do *Gal* Galician pasteurized cow's milk cheese
cecina salted & dried beef, rabbit or horse meat
    cecina de León Leonese cow's hind legs, salted, smoked & air-dried
cena evening meal (dinner, supper)
Cencibel = Tempranillo
centeno rye
    pan de **centeno** rye bread
centolla spider crab
centollo spider crab
cereal 1. cereal 2. grain
cerdeña Sardinian style
cerdo 1. pork 2. pig
    cerdo en lata canned pork luncheon meat
    cerdo para asar pork joint (for roasting)
    cerdo picada minced (ground) pork
~*Cerdo y patatas al estilo extremeño* Extremaduran style pork & potato casserole
cerezas cherries
cerrado closed (shop sign)
cerveza beer
    cerveza sin non-alcoholic beer
    cerveza sin alcohol non-alcoholic beer

chacina cured meat
chalota shallot

champiñones cultivated mushrooms
~Champiñones a la crema mushrooms with cream
~Champiñones al ajillo mushrooms sautéed with garlic
~Champiñones en salsa... mushrooms in ...sauce
~Champiñones salteados sautéed mushrooms
~Champiñones salteados con ajo = *Champiñónes al ajillo*
~Champiñones salteados en mantequilla mushrooms sautéed in butter
Chanfaina thick Extremaduran stew of lamb, offal (e.g. liver), bread, blood sausage, almonds, garlic, & vinegar; peppers, rice, hard-boiled eggs, potatoes, & beans can be added
chanquetes transparent gobies (whitebait)
~Chanquetes fritos fried whitebait
charcutería 1. meat curing 2. cured meat & cheese shop
cherna wreckfish (stone bass)
cherne de ley white grouper (fish)
chícharos split peas
chicharra flying gurnard (fish)
chicharro blue jack mackerel (fish)
Chicharrones 1. type of pork dish 2. pork crackling (skin)
~Chicharrones de Cádiz Cádiz style pork belly ***Tapa*** (see)
chili chili (chilli) pepper
    chili en polvo chili powder
    chili picante hot chili
Chilindrón Aragonese chicken or lamb stew with paprika & sweet peppers
chipirones 1. small squid 2. little cuttlefish
Chireta Aragonese 'haggis'
chirimoya cherimoya (custard apple)
chiringuito beachside bar
chirivía parsnip
chistorra red spicy pork sausage from Aragon, Navarra & the Basque country; often fried & served as a ***Tapa*** (see)
chivo kid (baby goat)
Chochifrito fried pork
choco cuttlefish
~Chocos con habas cuttlefish with broad beans
chocolate chocolate
    chocolate a la española Spanish hot chocolate

chocolate a la taza chocolate with starch for making hot chocolate
chocolate caliente hot chocolate
Chochos types of coated sweet
~*Chochos de Lorca* Murcian sugar-coated hazelnuts
~*Chochos de yema* Salamancan egg-based sweet
chopa black sea bream (fish)
chopitos little cuttlefish
~*Chopitos* fried battered little cuttlefish *Tapa* (see)
choricero tangy red pepper, often used in Basque cuisine
chorizo red (from paprika) pork sausage, obtainable spicy or mild, raw for cooking or ready to eat
~*Chorizo a la plancha* griddled chorizo
~*Chorizo a la riojana* = *Chorizo al vino* (below)
~*Chorizo a la sidra* chorizo slowly cooked in cider, often with added garlic, served as a *Tapa* (see)
~*Chorizo al vino* chorizo slowly cooked in red Rioja wine, served as a *Tapa* (see)
choto kid (baby goat)
~ *Choto ajillo a la granadina* Granada style kid stew with garlic
chucla 1. blotched picarel (fish) 2. bigeye picarel (fish)
chucleto Mediterranean sand smelt (fish)
chufas tiger nuts
chuleta 1. chop 2. cutlet
    chuleta de aguja pork shoulder chop
        chuletas de aguja lamb best end
    chuleta de cerdo pork chop
    chuleta de cordero lamb chop
    chuleta de lomo bajo con solomillo T-bone steak
    chuleta de pierna lamb chump chop
~*Chuletas de cerdo a la madrileña* Madrid style baked marinated pork chops
~*Chuletas de cordero a la navarra* Navarra style lamb chops with thick tomato-based sauce & **chorizo** (see)
~*Chuletas de cordero a la pamplona* Pamploma style lamb chops with **chorizo** (see)
~*Chuletas de cordero a la parrilla* grilled (broiled) lamb chops
~*Chuletas de cordero al jerez* lamb chops with sherry
chuletillas ribs

~*Chuletillas al sarmiento* La Rioja style lamb rib chops cooked over dried vine branch embers
chuletón large beef chop from rib roast (giant steak)
~*Chuletón a la vasca* Basque style grilled (broiled) beef chop
chumbo prickly pear cactus (fruit & stems)
Churrasco 1. grilled (broiled) meat (in general)
   2. Galician pork or beef spare ribs
~*Churrasco cordobés* Córdoban grilled meat with dipping sauces (sometimes with DIY grilling on hotplate)
Churros type of fried dough snack, often long, thick & ridged

cidra type of gourd
Ciegas de Íscar Valladolid puff buns
ciervo deer
cigala 1. Dublin Bay prawn (langoustine) 2. crayfish
   3. *Ctn* flat lobster
cigarra flat lobster
cilantro coriander
ciruela plum
    ciruelas damascenas damsons
    ciruelas pasas prunes
    ciruelas secadas prunes
ciurenys *Ctn* porcini mushroom

clauells de girofle *Ctn* cloves
clavell *Ctn* thornback ray (fish)
clavellada *Ctn* thornback ray (fish)
clavos cloves
clementina clementine

Coca (*plural* *Coques*) *Ctn* Catalan pastry with many variations, sweet & savoury
~*Coca de trampó* Mallorcan flatbread topped with vegetables
Cochifritos sautéed meat dishes
~*Cochifrito a la navarra* Navarra style sautéed lamb with lemon juice
cochinillo suckling pig
~*Cochinillo asado* roast suckling pig
cocido[1]/cocida cooked

Cocido[2] meat, vegetable & chickpea stew
~*Cocido madreleña* = *Cocido*[2] (above)
~*Cocido maragato* rich Castilian mixed meats, chickpeas & vegetable stew with dumplings
cocina 1. cuisine 2. kitchen
coco coconut
codillo knuckle
    codillo de cerdo pig's hock
codorniz (*plural* **codornices**) quail
~*Codornices asados* roast quails
~*Codornices emborrachadas* ('Drunken quail') quail cooked with wine & brandy
~*Cordonices en escabeche (Cordonices escabechadas)* pickled quails
~*Codornices en hojas de parra* baked or grilled (broiled) quail wrapped in vine leaves
~*Codornices con tomate* quails with tomato sauce
cogollo heart
    cogollos de palmito palm hearts
~*Cogollos al ajillo* Cordoban style garlic-fried romaine lettuce hearts
Cojodongo Extremaduran summer mixed salad with vegetables
Cojonuda Burgos style blood sausage with fried quail egg on a slice of bread, served as a *Tapa* (see)
Cojonudo as for *Cojonuda* (above) but **chorizo** (see) used in place of blood sausage
col cabbage
    coles de Bruselas Brussels' sprouts
~*Col blanca con ajoaceite* white cabbage with garlic sauce
~*Col rellena* cabbage leaves stuffed with meat
~*Coles a la catalana*i Catalan style cabbage with romesco sauce (see **salsa romesco**)
cola tail
    cola de vaca oxtail
~*Cola de vaca en caldo* oxtail in soup
coliflor cauliflower
~*Coliflor al ajiaceite* cauliflower with garlic sauce
~*Coliflor al ajo arriero* muleteer's style cauliflower with garlic

~*Coliflor empanada* fried breaded cauliflower
collejas bladder campion (Manchegan wild vegetable)
colorantes colourings (for food)
   sin **colorantes artificiales** without artificial colourings
colza rape seed
comedor basic restaurant with cheap set meals (diner)
comida 1. food 2. meal
   comida típica regional dish
comino cumin
con with
concha 1. shell 2. seashell 3. various shellfish
   concha de peregrino pilgrim scallop
   concha fina smooth clam
   sin las **conchas** without the shells
~*Conchas de atún* tuna (tunny) in scallop shells with scarlet sweet pepper sauce
conejo rabbit
~*Conejo a la cazadora* huntress' style rabbit with pork & ham
~*Conejo al ajillo* rabbit with garlic
~*Conejo con arroz* rabbit with rice
~*Conejo en adobo* casserole of marinated rabbit
~*Conejo en escabeche* soused rabbit
~*Conejo en salmorejo* Canarian rabbit stew with coriander
~*Conejo en salsa de almendras* rabbit in almond sauce
~*Conejo tarraconense* Tarragon style rabbit & potato stew
confitura 1. jam 2. preserve
congelado/congelada frozen
congre *Ctn* conger eel (fish)
cóngrio conger eel (fish)
~*Congrio a la riojana* conger eel with sweet peppers & red wine
~*Congrio con pasas y piñones* Mallorcan style conger eel stew with raisins & pine nuts
conill *Ctn* rabbit
conservantes preservatives
   sin **conservantes artificiales** without artificial preservatives
conservar en lugar fresco y seco store in a cool dry place
consomé consommé (rich clear soup)
   consomé de gallina chicken consommé

consomé madrileño beef consommé with diced tomatoes
consomé de pollo chicken consommé
consumir preferentemente antes del... consume before...
contiene contains
    contiene frutos secos contains nuts
    contiene gluten contains gluten
contra beef top rump
contramuslo thigh (poultry)
    contramuslos de pollo chicken thighs
    contramuslos de pollo deshuesados/sin hueso boneless chicken thighs
~*Contramuslos de pollo al horno con patatas* baked chicken thighs with potatoes
copa 1. glass (for wine) 2. cup
    copa de Navidad (Xmas cup) raisin infused anise brandy
    una **copa** *de...* a wine glass of...
~*Copa de frutas = Macedonia de frutas*
~*Copa imperial* coffee jelly (jello) with eggnog
copinya llisa *Ctn* carpet-shell (bivalve mollusc)
Coques see *Coca*
Coquetes Costa Blanca style 'pizza'
Coquillos de miel honey-drenched fried pastry
coquina wedge shell (bivalve mollusc)
~*Coquinas con arroz* wedge shells with rice
coquitos Brazil nuts
corazón heart
~*Corazones* ('Hearts') Cantabrian sweet
corba *Ctn* 1. brown meagre (fish) 2. shi drum (fish)
corball shi drum (fish)
corcón thick-lip grey mullet (fish)
cordero lamb
~*Cordero a la pastora* shepherdess' style marinated lamb & potato casserole
~*Cordero al chilindrón* Aragonese baby lamb with bell peppers
~*Cordero asado* roast lamb
~*Cordero en ajillo pastor* shepherd's style lamb stew with garlic
cordobés/cordobesa Cordoban style
cornet amb pues *Ctn* murex (single-shell mollusc)
cornuda *Ctn* hammerhead (fish)

cortado small strong version of coffee with milk
corvallo 1. brown meagre (fish) 2. shi drum (fish)
corvina meagre (fish)
~*Corvina en salsa de alcaparras* meagre in caper sauce
corzo roe deer
cosecha 1. vintage 2. harvest
costillar beef top rib
    costillar de cordero rack of lamb
    costillar y lomo saddle of lamb
~*Costillar de cordero a la parrilla* grilled (broiled) rack of lamb
costillas ribs
    costillas de cordero lamb rib chops
    costillas de ternera beef ribs
~*Costillas a la parrilla* grilled (broiled) pork spare ribs
~*Costillas al horno* baked pork spare ribs
~*Costillas con piña* Canarian pork spare ribs with corn on the cob (**piña de millo**)
~*Costillas de cordero asadas a la parrilla* grilled (broiled) lamb rib chops
costrado/costrada crusted
~*Costrada manchega* toast baked with cheese & egg topping
costrón crust
cotufas popcorn (Canaries)

cranc *Ctn* 1. crab 2. velvet swimming crab
    cranc pelut *Ctn* shore crab (= **cangrejo moruno**)
    cranc verd *Ctn* shore crab (= **cangrejo de mar**)
crema 1. cream 2. cream soup
    crema de queso 1. cream cheese 2. cheese spread
~*Crema catalana* Catalan custard dessert
~*Crema de Aranjuez* = *Crema de espárragos* (below)
~*Crema de espárragos* cream of asparagus soup
cremadina custard filling for cakes
Crespell Mallorcan biscuit (cookie)
criadillas testicles
    criadillas de tierra truffles
~*Criadillas de le tierra a la extremeña* Extremaduran style chopped truffles in sauce

~***Criadillas fritas*** fried testicles (pig's, lamb's or calve's)
crianza matured in oak (wine)
Cristinas de San Blas cream-filled buns from Lleida, Catalonia
croisant croissant
Croquetas croquettes, often of leftovers (shrimp, ham, etc.)
    enclosed in potato, breaded & deep-fried
~***Croquetas de bacalao*** salt cod & potato croquettes
~***Croquetas de jamón*** breaded croquettes with ham filling
~***Croquetas de pollo*** breaded shredded chicken croquettes
crosta *Ctn* crust
crudo/cruda raw
crujiente 1. crunchy 2. crispy

Cuajada 1. junket (dessert of milk plus rennet) 2. curd
cuajo rennet
Cuba Libre white rum & Coke, with or without lime juice
cubano/cubana Cuban style
cubata = **Cuba Libre**
cubiertos cutlery
cuchara spoon
cuchillo knife
cuello 1. neck 2. lamb neck 3. beef neck
    cuello de cordero neck of lamb
la **cuenta** the bill (check)
cuerno horn-shell (single-shell mollusc)
culata de contra beef top rump
Culeca type of Spanish cake of bread, resembling a
    donut, & topped with an egg; also contains **chorizo** (see)
curado/curada cured
cúrcuma turmeric

A Dictionary of Food in Spain

D

D.O
D.O.Ca } abbreviations indicating better quality wines
D.O.Q

dátil palm date

de (d') 1. of 2. from
del 1. of the 2. from the
dehesa de Extremadura Extremaduran dried aged ham
dentón dentex (fish)
~Dentón al horno baked dentex
~Dentón con salsa de almendras dentex with almond sauce
déntol *Ctn* dentex (fish)
desayuno breakfast
deshuesado/deshuesada 1. boneless 2. deboned 3. shelled

diente 1. clove (of garlic) 2. tooth
    diente de ajo clove of garlic

doncella rainbow wrasse (fish)
donostiarra San Sebastian style
dorada gilthead bream (fish)
~Dorada a la sal gilthead bream baked in salt
dorado dolphin fish
Dormido del corpus Toledo oval bun made with eggs, sugar, olive oil, flour & yeast; interior fluffy, exterior crunchy

dragó *Ctn* lizard fish

Duelos y quebrantos ('Duels & losses') Manchegan pan-fried dish of scrambled eggs, **chorizo** (see) & streaky bacon, often served in a clay pot
dulce 1. sweet 2. sweet preparation, pastry or pudding
    dulce de membrillo quince jelly

~***Dulce de batata*** sweet potato pudding

duro/dura hard

E

eglefino haddock (fish)

el the

emborrachado/emborrachada 1. drunk 2. cooked with wine or spirit
embotit *Ctn* = **embutido**
embuchado sausage
embutido cured dry sausage (many varieties)
Empanada[1] pasty (pastry with filling, hand pie)
~*Empanada de espinacas y queso* spinach & cheese pie
~*Empanada gallega...*   Galician pie (...various fillings):
    de anguila   eel
    de atún   tuna
    de bacalao   salt cod & raisins
    de bonito   bonito (fish)
    de carne   beef & **chorizo** (see)
    de lomo   pork
    de pollo   chicken
    de sardinas   sardines
Empanadilla small pasty (pastry with filling, hand pie)
~*Empanadilla de atún* small tuna pasty
~*Empanadilla de cebolla* small onion pasty
~*Empanadilla de espinacas* small spinach pasty
~*Empanadilla de tomate* small tomato pasty
empanado[1]/**empanada**[2] breaded
Empanado[2] breaded cutlet
~*Empanados de cerdo* fried breaded pork cutlets
Emparedados fried breaded ham & cheese sandwiches
emperador swordfish

en 1. in 2. at 3. on
    en escabeche 1. pickled 2. marinated
    en su punto ('just right') medium-rare (steak)

encargo 1. request 2. order
   por **encargo** by special order
encebollado/encebollada smothered in onions
endibia 1. endive 2. chicory
endrinas sloes
enebros juniper berries
eneldo dill weed
Ensaïmadas mallorquinas sweet or savoury Mallorcan buns
Ensalada salad
~*Ensalada de alcachofas* artichoke salad
~*Ensalada de judías verdes* green bean salad
~*Ensalada de pimientos* bell pepper (capsicum) salad
~*Ensalada de pimientos asados* roasted bell pepper salad
~*Ensalada de pulpo* octopus salad
~*Ensalada de San Isidro* lettuce & pickled or canned tuna
~*Ensalada de verduras* mixed cooked vegetable salad
~*Ensalada mixta* mixed salad
~*Ensalada rusa* Russian salad (elaborate potato salad)
~*Ensalada San Isidro = Ensalada de San Isidro*
~*Ensalada sevillana* Sevillian style escarole (type of endive), green olives & tarragon
Ensaladilla 1. Russian salad (elaborate potato salad) 2. salad
~*Ensaladilla de arroz* rice salad
~*Ensaladilla de patatas* potato salad
~*Ensaladilla rusa* Russian salad (elaborate potato salad)
entero/entera whole
entraña beef skirt (diaphragm)
~*Entraña a la parrilla* grilled (broiled) beef skirt
Entrantes starters
entrecot beef sirloin steak
Entremeses 1. hors d'oeuvres 2. appetizers 3. starters

erizo hedgehog
   erizo de mar sea urchin

escabechado/escabechada 1. pickled 2. marinated
escabeche marinade
   en **escabeche** 1. pickled 2. marinated
~*Escabeche de berenjena* pickled aubergine (eggplant)

~Escabeche de boquerones soused anchovies
~Escabeche de pescado marinated fish (various)
escabetx *Ctn* = **escabeche** (above)
Escalibada Catalan salad of roasted bell peppers & roasted aubergines (eggplants)
Escalivada *Ctn* = *Escalibada* (above)
escalo bordallo (fish)
escalonia shallot
Escalopes de ternera labrador farmer's style schnitzels of veal slices sandwiched between ham slices
escamarlà *Ctn* Dublin Bay prawn (langoustine)
escarola 1. escarole 2. endive
escat *Ctn* monkfish (angel-fish)
escolà *Ctn* Spanish ling (fish)
escolano greater forkbeard (fish)
escopinya *Ctn* types of bivalve mollusc
    escopinya de gallet *Ctn* cockle
    escopinya gravada *Ctn* warty Venus
escorball *Ctn* brown meagre (fish)
escorpión greater weever (fish)
Escudella i carn d'olla *Ctn* complex mixed meats & vegetable stew, with the resultant soup served first with noodles
Esgarraet *Ctn* Valencian grilled (broiled) red pepper salad with salt cod, garlic, olive oil & sometimes black olives
espadín sprat (fish)
espagueti spaghetti
español/española Spanish style
Españoletas Aragonese cookies
espárrago 1. asparagus 2. docked lamb's tail (Aragon)
    espárragos blancos white asparagus
~Espárragos a la andaluza Andalusian style asparagus with garlic, cumin & eggs
~Espárragos gratinados asparagus with grated cheese
~Espárragos montañeses Aragonese docked lambs' tails, stewed & fried
esparrall *Ctn* annular bream (fish)
especia spice
especial 1. special 2. house special

Espencat *Ctn* Valencian roasted vegetable salad, typically with bell peppers & aubergines (eggplants)
espet *Ctn* barracuda (fish)
espetón 1. skewer 2. spit (for cooking) 3. barracuda (fish)
Espetos skewered charcoal-grilled (broiled) sardines
espinaca spinach
~*Espinacas a la cordobesa* Cordoban style spinach with garlic, paprika, cinnamon & vinegar
~*Espinacas con garbanzos* spinach with chickpeas
espuma 1. mousse 2. scum on broth 3. beer froth (head)
~*Espuma de fruta* fruit mousse
Esqueixada *Ctn* salad of raw shredded salt cod, tomatoes, onions, olive oil & vinegar; sometimes with aubergine (eggplant), bell peppers & a garnish of hard-boiled eggs or olives
~*Esqueixada de bacallà* *Ctn* = *Esqueixada*
estilo style
   al **estilo...** in the...style
estofado[1]/estofada stewed
Estofado[2] stew
~*Estofado a la andaluza* Andalusian style beef (or veal) & vegetable stew
~*Estofado de buey a la asturiana* Asturian style beef stew with calf's foot & vegetables
~*Estofado de lengua* braised pig's tongue
~*Estofado de ternera con patatas* beef stew with potatoes
estorión sturgeon (fish)
estornino chub mackerel (fish)
estragón tarragon

Etxeko bixkotxa *Bsq* Basque gateau with cream filling

extremeño/extremeña Extremaduran style

F

Fabada = *Fabada asturiana* (below)
~*Fabada asturiana* Asturian style rich pork & bean stew
fabes dried large white Asturian runner beans
    for *Fabada* (above)
~*Fabes con almejas* Asturian bean & clam stew
~*Fabes con amasueles* = *Fabes con almejas* (above)
faisán pheasant
~*Faisán al modo de Alcántara* braised port-marinated stuffed
    pheasant with truffles, the Alcántara (Extremadura) way
falda 1. beef flank 2. breast of lamb
~*Falda rellena* stuffed beef flank
falso/falsa false
    falso abadejo 1. goldblotch grouper (fish)
                       2. blacktip grouper
Fartons *Ctn* Valencian sponge fingers for dipping in a tiger
    nut drink, hot chocolate or milky coffee
fava (*plural* **faves**) *Ctn* broad bean
~*Fava parada* *Ctn* Balearic complex soup of broad beans,
    vegetables, pork, pig's trotters, blood sausage & noodles
~*Faves al tombet* *Ctn* Alicante style broad beans with lettuce

fecha de caducidad use-by date
feira *Gal* fair (festive)
    á **feira** *Gal* fair style
Feos ('Ugly ones') almond cookies from Castille-León
fesols de Santa Pau *Ctn* type of white bean from Garrotxa

Fiambre 1. cold meat 2. pressed meat 3. pâté
~*Fiambre de bonito* bonito (fish) pâté
fideo vermicelli noodle
~*Fideos a la catalana* Catalan style casserole of noodles, pork
    & sausage
Fideuà *Ctn* = *Cazuela de fideos*
Figues albardaes Valencian fig fritters

filete 1. slice of steak, veal or pork 2. beef fillet steak 3. fillet (fish or chicken)
   filete de ternera fillet steak (filet mignon)
~***Filetes a la casera*** home style veal cutlets with garlic
~***Filetes a la plancha*** griddled pork cutlets with garlic
Filloas Galician dessert crêpes
fino[1] dry sherry
fino[2]/**fina** 1. fine 2. thin 3. slender 4. smooth

Flamenquines Andalusian fried breaded ham & pork roll-ups
Flan 1. caramel custard dessert 2. other custards
~***Flan de tomate*** tomato custard savoury starter
Flaó (*plural ***Flaons***) *Ctn* 1. Balearic cheesecake or tart
   2. ***Flaons*** = ***Pastissets***
flor flower
   Flor de Guía, queso de Canarian cheese from ewe's milk, with added cow's milk or goat's milk
~***Flores de hojaldre*** flower-shaped puff pastry cakes, usually sweet, sometimes savory

forn *Ctn* oven
   al forn *Ctn* baked

frambuesas raspberries
Frangollo Canarian dessert with eggs, sugar, raisins & almonds
freír to fry
   ***para* freír** for frying
fresas strawberries
fresones strawberries
Fricandó Catalan beef stew with mushrooms
frijoles dried beans
frío/fría cold
Frisuelos Asturian & Leonese style dessert crêpes
frito[1]/**frita** fried
Fritos[2] 1. fried foods 2. fritters
~***Fritos de espinacas*** spinach fritters
fritura fried food
~***Fritura de pecados*** mixed fish fry
Frixuelos = ***Frisuelos***

fruta fruit
~***Frutas de Aragón*** Aragonese fruit confit covered in chocolate
fruto seco nut (any)
    frutos secos 1. nuts (any) 2. nuts & dried fruits

fuego 1. heat 2. flame
    a **fuego lento** over a low heat
fuerte strong
fuet *Ctn* dry-cured Catalan pork sausage

A Dictionary of Food in Spain

G

Gachas porridge or gruel of various regional styles, often served with pork products: bacon, liver, blood sausage, etc.
~***Gachas dulces*** Andalusian sweet porridge dessert
~***Gachas extremeñas*** Extremaduran porridge dessert with anis
gaditano/gaditana Cádiz style
galera mantis shrimp
Galianos* = *Gaszpachos manchegos
gall *Ctn* John dory (fish)
gallano cuckoo wrasse (fish)
gallego/gallega Galician style
Galleta biscuit (cookie)
~***Galletas de Pepa Niebla*** anise brandy biscuits
~***Galletas Maria*** thin sweet biscuits
gallina hen
~***Gallina en pebre*** hen casserole with garlic sauce
~***Gallina en pepitoria*** hen casserole with almonds
~***Gallina rellena*** gently stewed stuffed hen
gallineta 1. blackbelly rosefish 2. red scorpionfish 3. small red scorpionfish 4. slender rockfish 5. *Ctn* red gurnard (fish)
gallo 1. cock (poultry) 2. four-spot megrim (fish) 3. megrim (fish) 4. John dory (fish)
~***Gallo al limon*** baked megrim with lemon
galludo 1. longnose spurdog (fish) 2. picked dogfish
galta pig's cheek
galta-roig *Ctn* golden grey mullet (fish)
galúa leaping mullet (fish)
galupe 1. golden grey mullet (fish) 2. flathead grey mullet 3. thinlip grey mullet 4. white mullet 5. bluespot mullet
gamba prawn (shrimp)
    gambas cocidas cooked prawns
    gambas crudas raw prawns
    gambas d'esquer *Ctn* brown shrimp
    gambas peladas peeled prawns
    gambas rosadas red prawns

~*Gambas a la plancha* griddled prawns
~*Gambas al ajillo* prawns sautéed with garlic
~*Gambas al pil pil* sizzling garlic & chili prawns
~*Gambas rebozadas* deep-fried battered prawns
gambeta *Ctn* common prawn (shrimp)
gambón prawn (shrimp)
    gambón gigante very large prawn
    gambón grande large prawn
Gamonéu, queso de (Gamonedo) lightly smoked Asturian cheese from a blend of cow's, goat's & ewe's milk
Gañote Extremaduran fried spiral sweet pastry
ganso gander
garapiñado/garapiñada sugar-coated (candied)
garbanzos chickpeas
    garbanzos de Escacena high quality chickpeas
    garbanzos de Fuentesaúco high quality chickpeas
Garbure navarro Navarra style pork & vegetable soup
Garnacha red & white wine grapes
garneo piper gurnard (fish)
garneu *Ctn* piper gurnard (fish)
garrafón type of butter bean (white lima bean)
gat *Ctn* lesser-spotted dogfish
gató *Ctn* large-spotted dogfish (huss)
gatvaire *Ctn* large-spotted dogfish (huss)
Gazpacho 1. Andalusian cold tomato soup 2. other soups of raw blended vegetables, usually cold
~*Gazpacho andaluz* Andalusian cold tomato soup
~*Gazpacho blanco con huevos* cold white soup with eggs
~*Gazpacho caliente* hot tomato soup
~*Gazpacho de aguacates* cold avocado soup
~*Gazpacho de mango* cold mango soup
Gazpachos rustic stew
~*Gaszpachos manchegos* La Mancha style shepherd's rabbit & partridge stew
Gazpachuelo Málaga style basic fisherman's soup of bread, garlic, olive oil, egg & potatoes, served hot; some versions contain shellfish

Gelat *Ctn* ice cream

Gelatina jelly (jello)
germen germ (grain)
    germen de trigo wheatgerm
gerret *Ctn* picarel (fish)

gibelurdiña Russula virescens (Basque wild mushroom)
Gildas = Banderillas
ginebre ginger
girasol sunflower
Girella = Chireta
Gireta = Chireta
gitanillo 1. gypsy girl or boy 2. gypsy girl style
gitano 1. gypsy style 2. mottled grouper (fish)
    3. island grouper (fish)

globito little cuttlefish

gòbit *Ctn* goby (fish)
Godello grape from N.W. Spain producing rich dry white wines
gofio Canarian flour of roasted grains
golondrina de mar flying fish
gordo/gorda thick

gramos grams
gran reserva term for a wine from an outstanding vintage,
    aged for minimum of 5 years (2 years in oak)
granada pomegranate
granadina[1] 1. grenadine syrup
    2. meat cutlet larded with strips of ham
~Granadinas de ternera granadines of veal with mushrooms
granadino/granadina[2] Granada style
granel ('bulk cargo') loose (unpackaged) fruit & vegetables
granizado summer drink with crushed ice & sugar
    granizado de café coffee ice, with or without brandy
    granizado de limón lemon ice
    granizado de vino wine or sherry ice with orange juice
grasa fat
gratinado/gratinada 1. grated (cheese)
    2. with grated cheese (au gratin)

Greixera de macarones *Ctn* macaroni, cheese & egg casserole
Greixonera Balearic type of sweet bread pudding
~***Greixonera de brosat*** *Ctn* Mallorcan cheese cake
grelos turnip leaves
grevi *Ctn* type of Balearic sauce, similar to gravy in consistency
grimalt *Ctn* lobster
grosellas 1. currants (black, red or white) 2. otaheite gooseberry
    grosellas espinosas gooseberries

guardia civil hammerhead (fish)
guayaba guava
guindas 1. cherries 2. morello cherries
~***Guindas en anis*** cherries in anise brandy
guindillas hot chili peppers
guingueta *Ctn* beachside bar
Guirlache Aragonese almond brittle sweet (candy)
guisado/guisada 1. stewed 2. casseroled
guisantes peas
~***Guisantes a la leridana*** Lleida style peas with pork & sausage
~***Guisantes a la valenciana*** Valencian style peas with wine & anise brandy
~***Guisantes en salsa*** peas in sauce, topped with chopped egg
guisar to stew
    para **guisar** for stewing
guiso stew
guitarra guitar fish

H

habas broad beans
~Habas a la asturiana Asturian style broad beans with vegetables & wine
~Habas a la catalana Catalan style broad beans with pork, sausage & black (blood) pudding
~Habas a la montañesa Cantabrian style broad bean casserole with bacon, ham & bell peppers
~Habas a la rondeña Ronda style broad beans with ham & eggs
~Habas con calzones ('Broad beans with breeches') young broad beans in their shells, stringed, boiled & fried with garlic
~Habas con chocos = *Chocos con habas*
~Habas con jamón broad beans with ham & garlic
habichuelas 1. French beans 2. kidney beans
Hamburguesa de ternera beefburger (hamburger)
harina flour
    harina con levadura self-raising flour
    harina de trigo plain wheat flour

hecho done
    bien **hecho** well-done (steak)
    muy **hecho** well-done (steak)
    poco **hecho** cooked rare (steak)
Helado ice cream
~Helado al oloroso sherry ice cream
~Helado de chocolate chocolate ice cream
~Helado de fresa strawberry ice cream
~Helado de nata cream ice cream
~Helado de turrón nougat ice cream
~Helado de vainilla vanilla ice cream
Herbero Alicante region alcoholic herbal liquor
herrera striped bream (fish)
Hervido = *Bollit*

hielo ice
    con **hielo** with ice
    sin **hielo** without ice

hierba herb
    hierba luisa lemon verbena
    con **hierbas** with herbs
    hierbas provenzales mixed herbs
hierbabuena 1. mint 2. spearmint
higadillo liver (of small animals, especially birds)
~Higadillos salteados sautéed chicken livers
hígado liver (minly used are pig's & lamb's)
    hígado de cerdo pig's liver
    hígado de cordero lamb's liver
    hígado de pollo chicken livers
~Hígado a la asturiana Liver & bacon Asturian style
~Hígado al vino tinto sautéed liver with red wine sauce
~Hígado con salsa de almendras liver in almond sauce
~Hígado en adobo liver in sour sauce
higo fig
    higo chumbo prickly pear cactus (fruit & stems)
~Higos a la malagueña Málaga style fresh figs with wine & lemon juice
~Higos en salsa almendras figs in almond sauce, warm or cold
hinojo fennel

hojaldre puff pastry
~Hojaldres de Astorga Leonese sweet puff pastries
hojas de parra vine leaves
hojuelas sweet fried batter
hongo 1. fungus 2. types of wild mushroom
horchata cold tiger nut 'milk'
Hornazo (Hornazo castellano) Castilian style meat pie made of flour & yeast pastry, stuffed with pork loin, hard-boiled eggs & spicy **chorizo** (see)
horno oven
    al **horno** oven-baked

huerta garden

hueso bone
>*sin* **hueso** boneless

~*Huesos de santo* ('Saint's bones') cylindrical almond sweets for All Saints Day

huevas roe

~*Huevas de pescado* poached & fried fish roe

huevo egg
>**huevos camperos** free range eggs
>**huevos de cordoniz** quail eggs
>**huevos de pato** duck eggs

~*Huevos al plato** eggs served in the same dish in which they have been cooked (often baked) : here see *a la flamenca*, a la vasca*, en nido de espinacas*, en nido de patatas*, tórtola valenciana**

~*Huevos a la cordobesa* Cordoban style fried eggs with potatoes & **chorizo** (see)

~*Huevos a la flamenca** Andalusian baked egg & vegetable dish; many variants, some with added ham & **chorizo** (see)

~*Huevos a la vasca** Basque eggs with asparagus & peas

~*Huevos a la vizcaína* Biscay hard-boiled eggs with tomato

~*Huevos al modo de Soller* Mallorcan fried eggs with red Mallorcan sausage & peas

~*Huevos arriba España* egg & cheese on toast, baked

~*Huevos bechamel empanados* fried breaded poached eggs with bechamel sauce

~*Huevos duros* hard-boiled eggs

~*Huevos empanados* fried breaded poached eggs

~*Huevos en nido de espinacas** eggs baked in spinach nests

~*Huevos en nido de patatas** eggs baked in potato nests

~*Huevos en salsa de almendras* hard-boiled eggs in almond sauce

~*Huevos estrellados* ('Star eggs') = *Huevos rotos* (below)

~*Huevos fritos* fried eggs

~*Huevos hilados* candied egg threads

~*Huevos mole* rich egg-based Canarian dessert

~*Huevos rellenos* stuffed eggs (various stuffings)

~*Huevos rellenos de marisco* eggs stuffed with shellfish

~*Huevos revueltos* scrambled eggs

~*Huevos revueltos con espárragos* scrambled eggs with asparagus

~*Huevos rotos* fried eggs with broken runny yoke; many different accompaniments, including French fries
~*Huevos rotos con chistorra y patatas* broken fried eggs with potatoes & **chistorra** (see) sausage
~*Huevos serrranos* mountain style fried eggs on ham-filled halved tomatoes, sprinkled with grated cheese
~*Huevos tórtola valenciana** ('Turtle dove eggs') Valencian baked eggs with topping of artichokes, hen's liver, cheese
hurta 1. bluespotted sea bream (fish) 2. redbanded sea bream

I

i *Ctn* and

ibérico/ibérica from the Iberian pig (black pig)
Ibores, queso Extremaduran ubpasteurized goat's milk cheese

Idiazabal, queso Basque pressed unpasteurized ewe's milk cheese

infusión herbal tea
    infusión de manzanilla chamomile tea
    infusión de tila lime blossom tea
Intxaursalsa *Bsq* Basque Christmas Eve walnut cream soup

Izarra Basque liqueur

A Dictionary of Food in Spain

J

jabalí boar
~*Jabalí a la montañesa* Cantabrian style wild boar
Jabugo dried aged ham from Huelva
jamón ham (see also **dehesa, Jabugo, lacón, Los Pedroches**)
   jamón serrano salted, dried & aged ham (most popular) :
      jamón de cebo fodder fed
      jamón de la pata ('ham from the leg') ham off the bone
      jamón ibérico from black pigs (more expensive)
      jamón ibérico de bellota same fed on acorns (dearest)
      jamón serrano hembra from a female pig
   jamón de Séron dried aged ham from Séron, Almería
   jamón de Travélez dried aged ham from Granada
   jamón York ordinary ham
   jamón al horno baked ham off the bone
~*Jamón a lo gitanillo* gypsy girl style serrano ham with sweet & sour sauce
~*Jamón al jerez* ordinary ham with sherry
~*Jamón con melón o higos* cold serrano ham with melon or figs
jamoncitos de pollo chicken legs
japuta Ray's bream (fish)
jarabe syrup
jareas Canarian salted & sun-dried small fish (various)
jarra 1. carafe 2. jug

jengibre ginger
jerez[1] sherry
Jerez[2] sherry wine region (see map, p.117)

jibia cuttlefish
~*Jibia en salsa* cuttlefish in sauce
Jijona type of nougat from Jijona (Valencia)

joven young

Juan García red wine grape

judías beans
    judías anchas ('wide beans') flat stringless green beans
    judías secas dried beans
    judías verdes French beans
    judías verdes anchas = **judías anchas** (above)
~*Judías a la madrileña* = *Judías a lo tío Lucas* (below)
~*Judías a lo tío Lucas* Madrid style Uncle Lucas' dried white bean stew with salt pork or bacon
~*Judías verdes a la castellana* Castilian style French beans with garlic, parsley & bell peppers (capsicums)
~*Judías verdes a la española* = *Judías verdes a la castellana*
~*Judías verdes salteadas* sautéed French beans
judío/judía Jewish style
judiones de la Granja type of large white or yellowish dried bean
julia rainbow wrasse (fish)
Jumilla wine region, mainly in Murcia (see map, p.117)
jurel horse mackerel (fish)

K

kaki persimmon
kalimotxo *Bsq* Basque drink of red wine mixed with cola

kilo kilogram
    medio **kilo** half a kilo
    un **kilo** one kilo
kiwi kiwi fruit

Kokotxas *Bsq* expensive Basque fish stew, utilizing hake throat flesh or cod cheeks
~***Kokotxas en salsa verde a la donostiarra*** the former dish San Sebastian style with green sauce
Koskera *Bsq* Basque style hake with green sauce

A Dictionary of Food in Spain

L

L'Alt Urgell y La Cerdanya, queso de Catalan pasturized cow's milk cheese
la the
    la cuenta the bill (check)
    La Gomera Canarian raw goat's milk cheeses, sometimes with added ewe's milk; soft, cured or semi-cured
    La Leyenda La Mancha raw ewe's milk cheese aged for 1 year
    La Mancha wine region (see map, p.117)
    La Peral Asturian blue ewe's & cow's milk cheese
    La Retorta Extremaduran raw ewe's milk cheese
    La Retorta mini smaller version of the former
    La Selva, queso de cow's milk cheese from near Girona
    La Serena, queso de Badajoz raw ewe's milk cheese, coagulated with wild milk thistle rennet
~*La bomba* large deep-fried breaded beef meatball encased in potato, & served as a *Tapa* (see)
labrador farmer's style
lacón dried ham from the pig's shoulder (see also **jamón**)
    lacón gallego Galician shoulder ham
~*Lacón con grelos* Galician style cured pork shoulder with turnip tops
Lagunillas Valladolid cakes with marzipan
laminado/laminada sliced
láminas fine slices
lamprea de mar sea lamprey
langosta spiny lobster
    langosta mora pink spiny lobster
~*Langosta a la catalana* Catalan style spiny lobster casserole, with or without chocolate
~*Langosta a la Costa Brava* Costa Brava style lobster casserole
langostino 1. large prawn (shrimp) 2. king prawn
    langostino de rio crayfish

langostino moruno large red prawn
~Langostinos a la plancha large griddled prawns
~Langostinos a la española Spanish style braised large prawns with garlic & white wine
~Langostinos a la vinagreta levantina cooked large prawns marinated in eastern vinaigrette
~Langostinos con arroz large prawns with rice
~Langostinos en salsa marinera large prawns in garlic, tomato & white wine sauce
~Langostinos salteados sautéed large prawns
lapa limpet (shellfish)
largo a good amount
    largo de café strong white- coffee
    largo de leche milky white coffee
las the
    Las Alpujarras, queso de Andalusian goat's milk cheese
lata tin (can)
latilla small tin (can)
laurel bay leaf
Lazos de San Guillermo Leonese puff pastry sweets

lechal suckling (piglet, calf or lamb)
lechazo young lamb
~Lechazo asado = Lechazo asado al estilo castellano (below)
~Lechazo asado al estilo castellano Castilian style roast baby lamb
leche milk
    leche con calcio milk enriched with calcium
    leche condensada condensed milk
    leche de cabra goat's milk
    leche de oveja sheep's milk
    leche de soja soya milk
    leche desnatada skimmed milk
    leche entera whole milk
    leche semidesnatada semi-skimmed milk
~Leche asada Canarian 'roasted milk' dessert custard
~Leche frita ('Fried milk') fried squares of dough made from milk, flour & sugar; served with sugar glaze & cinnamon
lechona *Ctn* piglet

lechuga lettuce
legumbre 1. vegetable 2. legume 3. pulse
lengua tongue
~*Lengua con nueces* veal tongue with walnut sauce
~*Lenguas con salsa de granadas* pigs' tongues with pomegranate sauce
lenguado* sole   [*general term for various species of this fish]
~*Lenguado a la gaditana* Cádiz style fried floured sole
~*Lenguado a la vasca* Basque style sole with sauce
lentejas lentils
Leonora Leonese pasteurized goat's milk cheese
leridano/leridana Lleida style
levadura leavening
    levadura en polvo 1. baking powder 2. dried yeast
    levadura prensada cake yeast (compressed wet yeast)
levantino/levantina Levantine style

liadillo little parcel
~*Liadillos sevillanos* Sevillian style meat-stuffed cabbage rolls
Liébana, quesucos de Cantabrian smoked or unsmoked cow's milk cheese, sometimes with added ewe's or goat's milk
liebre hare
~*Liebre estofado a la castellana* Castilian style hare stew
lima lime
limanda lemon sole
limón lemon
limonada de miel lemonade with honey
limpio/limpia 1. gutted & dressed (poultry) 2. clean
lingote type of dried bean
lisa* grey mullet   [*general term for all grey mullets]
~*Lisa en ajillo* grilled (broiled) grey mullet with garlic
~*Lisa en amarillo* grey mullet in saffron sauce
listado skipjack (fish)
Listan Negro Canarian red wine grape
litro litre (liter)
    medio **litro** half a litre
    un **litro** one litre

llagosta *Ctn* spiny lobster

llampuga *Ctn* dolphin fish
llisera *Ctn* flathead grey mullet (fish)
lliseria megrim (fish)
llissa* *Ctn* grey mullet   [*general term for all grey mullets]
llobarro *Ctn* European sea bass (fish)
llop *Ctn* European sea bass (fish)
lloro *Ctn* male cuckoo wrasse (fish)
lluç *Ctn* hake (fish)
llúcera *Ctn* blue whiting (fish)

Locro de maiz Galician style stewed corn (maize)
lombarda red cabbage
~Lombarda a la castellana Castilian style red cabbage
lomo loin (especially pork)
    lomo alto beef ribeye steak
    lomo bajo beef sirloin
    lomo de cerdo pork loin
~Lomo a la malagueña pork loin with sweet Málaga wine
~Lomo a la sal pork loin baked in salt crust
~Lomo con leche pork loin simmered in milk
~Lomo de cerdo a la aragonesa Aragonese style pork loin cooked with wine
~Lomo de cerdo relleno a la gaditana Cádiz style stuffed pork loin
~Lomo en adobo roasted marinated pork loin
lonchas slices
    lonchas finas thin slices
    lonchas gordas thick slices
longaniza long thin pork sausage with black pepper & other spices, such as nutmeg
los the
    Los Beyos, queso de Asturian cow's, goat's or sheep's milk cheese
    Los Pedroches Cordoban dried aged ham

lubina European sea bass (fish)
~Lubina a la asturiana Asturian style sea bass, baked with wine or cider

~***Lubina con gibelurdiñas*** sea bass with Basque country wild mushrooms (Russula virescens)
~***Lubina con salsa de cangrejos de rio*** sea bass with river crayfish sauce
~***Lubina en salsa verde*** sea bass in green sauce
lucio northern pike (fish)
luna moon

A Dictionary of Food in Spain

M

mabre *Ctn* striped bream (fish)
Macabeo grape producing still & sparkling white wines
Macarronada = *Macarrons amb grevi* (below)
macarrones macaroni
~*Macarrones a la española* Spanish style macaroni with bell peppers, ham & **chorizo** (see)
Macarrons amb grevi *Ctn* Balearic baked penne pasta with minced (ground) pork or beef, cheese & sauce
Macedonia 1. fruit salad 2. Macedonia
~*Macedonia de frutas* fresh fruit salad dessert
~*Macedonia de frutas de primavera* spring fruit cup
~*Macedonia de frutas de verano* summer fruit cup
macis mace
madrileño/madrileña Madrid style
Magdalenas sweet anise-scented muffins
magra[1] rasher (thin slice of bacon or ham)
~*Magras con tomate* sliced ham with tomato sauce
magro[1]**/magra**[2] lean
magro[2] sliced or cubed lean pork loin
~*Magro con tomate* fried cubed pork with tomato sauce
Mahón, queso de Menorcan cow's milk cheese
mahonesa mayonnaise
maire *Ctn* blue whiting (fish)
maíz corn (maize)
    maíz dulce sweetcorn
Majorero, queso de Fuerteventuran (Canarian) unpasteurized goat's milk semi-hard cheese
malagueño/malagueña Málaga style
Mallorca, queso Mallorcan cow's, goat's &/or ewe's milk cheese
mallorquín/mallorquina Mallorcan style
malva hibiscus flower
Malvasía grape producing sweet white wines

Manchego[1] sheep's milk cheese from La Mancha
    Manchego curado aged for 3-6 months
    Manchego fresca very young cheese
    Manchego semicurado aged for 3 weeks to 4 months
    Manchego viejo aged 1-2 years
manchego[2]**/manchega** La Mancha style
mandarina tangerine
manitas feet of animals
    manitas de cerdo pig's trotters
    manitas de cordero lamb shank
manojo 1. handful 2. bunch
manteca lard
Mantecadas mufffin-like sponge cakes
Mantecados shortbread cookies
mantequilla butter
    mantequilla con sal salted butter
    mantequilla sin sal unsalted butter
Manto Negro Balearic red wine grape
manzana apple
~*Manzanas asadas al vino* apples baked in wine
~*Manzanas rellenas* baked stuffed apples
manzanilla 1. chamomile 2. wine like dry fino sherry
mar sea
~*Mar i montanya* *Ctn* ('Sea & mountain') Catalan seafood with meat dishes
~*Mar i terra* *Ctn* ('Sea & land') Catalan chicken with lobster
maragota ballan wrasse (fish)
marconas almonds (special type)
margarina margerine
margarita type of carpet-shell (bivalve mollusc)
marinero/marinera sailor's style
marisco shellfish
Marmita = *Marmitako*
Marmitako *Bsq* Basque style tuna & potato casserole
maruca ling (fish)
masa 1. pastry dough 2. bread dough
    masa para empanada yeast pastry
matadero slaughterhouse
matalahúva (matalahúga) aniseed

Mató *Ctn* Catalan sweet, unsalted, unfermented, fresh cow's milk cheese, often served as a dessert with jam or honey
~*Mató de monja* = *Mató de Pedralbes* (below)
~*Mató de Pedralbes* *Ctn* type of Catalan custard dessert
~*Mató i mel* *Ctn* fresh cheese dessert with honey
mayonesa mayonnaise
    mayonesa a la andaluza Andalusian mayonnaise
mazapán marzipan

mechado/mechada larded
medio/media half
    media botella half-bottle
    media ración half portion (of dish)
    medio kilo half a kilo
    medio litro half a litre (liter)
~*Medias lunas* half-moon shaped biscuits
mejillones mussels
~*Mejillones a la marinera* sailor's style mussels with wine, parsley & garlic
~*Mejillones al vapor* steamed mussels
~*Mejillones en escabeche* pickled mussels
~*Mejillones rellenos* stuffed mussels *Tapa* (see)
mejorana marjoram
mel *Ctn* honey
~*Mel i mató* = *Mató i mel*
melaza molasses
meleta sprat (fish)
melocotón peach
melón melon
melva frigate mackerel (fish)
mèlvera frigate mackerel (fish)
membrillo quince
~*Membrillo cocido* quince compote with wine & spices
Mencía red wine grape
Menestra vegetable stew or casserole
~*Menestra de legumbres frescas* Murcian style fresh vegetable casserole with eggs
~*Menestra de verduras* Navarra style mixed vegetable casserole
Menjar blanc (Menjablanc) *Ctn* blancmange (almond pudding)

menta mint
menú = **menú del día**
    menú del día dish of the day (lunchtime)
Menudo tripe stew
~*Menudo gitano* Andalusian gypsy style tripe stew with pig's trotters & chickpeas
mercado market
Merienda any sweet or savoury late-afternoon light snack
merlan whiting
merlo brown wrasse (fish)
merluza hake (fish)
~*Merluza a la andaluza* Andalusian style hake with wine & nuts
~*Merluza a la bilbaína* Bilbao style hake with red bell peppers
~*Merluza a la koskera* = *Merluza en salsa verde* (below)
~*Merluza a la vasca* = *Merluza en salsa verde* (below)
~*Merluza con uvas* hake with grapes
~*Merluza con mayonesa* poached hake with mayonnaise
~*Merluza en salsa verde* Basque style hake in green sauce
~*Merluza rellena* stuffed hake
mermelada 1. jam 2. marmalade
    mermelada de fruta fruit jam
mero grouper (fish)
~*Mero a la naranja* grouper with orange sauce
~*Mero a la vinagreta* flaked poached grouper mixed with eggs, olives, capers, vinegar & olive oil; served cold
~*Mero con salsa de almendras* grouper with almond sauce
mesón rustic inn
mesonera hostess style
mezcla mixture

microonda microwave
miel honey
    miel de caña molasses
mielga spur dog (fish)
miga 1. little bit 2. crumb
~*Migas* basically a dish of fried breadcrumbs, to which are added such things as garlic & bacon or **chorizo** (see); fried breadcrumbs may also be eaten with sardines as a

Tapa (see); in S.E. Spain, a flour & water mix is substituted for breadcrumbs (***Migas de harina***)
mijo millet
mixto/mixta mixed

modo way (manner)
    al **modo de** in the way of
moixo *Ctn* sand smelt (fish)
mojama cured tuna
mojarra two-banded bream (fish)
Mojete Murcian salad of roasted bell peppers & roasted onions
mojo Canarian sauce
    mojo colorado Canarian red sauce with paprika, chili, cumin & vinegar
    mojo con queso mojo sauce with cheese
    mojo de almendras mojo with almonds
    mojo de azafrán mojo with saffron
    mojo verde Canarian green sauce, with parsley & coriander (cilantro) instead of paprika
moll *Ctn* types of red mullet (fish)
    moll de fang red mullet
    moll roquer surmullet
molleja 1. sweetbread (of cattle) 2. gizzard (of poultry)
~*Mollejas al oloroso* sweetbreads with oloroso sherry
mòllera *Ctn* forkbeard (fish)
mollete Andalusian flatbread
Mona de Pasqua rich Catalan pastry with almonds & chocolate
Monastrell grape producing powerful red wines
mondeju *Bsq* **(mondejo)** yellowish Basque sausage of mutton, vegetables & eggs
mongetes *Ctn* Catalan dried white beans
~*Mongetes amb botifarra* *Ctn* beans & pork sausage
Montaditos open-faced sandwiches with various toppings, served as *Tapas* (see)
montañeso/montañesa 1. highlander 2. Cantabrian
Monte Enebro pasteurized semi-cured goat's milk cheese, covered in grey & black mould

moras blackberries
morado purple
moraga bundle
~*Moraga de sardinas* sardine casserole
~*Moraga de sardinas a la granadina* Granada style sardine casserole
~*Moraga de sardinas a la malagueña* Málaga style sardine casserole
morcilla 1. blood sausage (black pudding) 2. sausage
    morcilla blanca de Jaén bloodless white Jaén sausage with pork from the pig's head & other meats
    morcilla de Burgos blood sausage from Burgos with onions & rice
    morcilla de Granada pork & blood sausage from Granada
    morcilla patatera Extremaduran pork & potato sausage
morcillo posterior (morcillo) beef shank
morcón sausage of lean pork with paprika & garlic
morena moray eel
morisco/morisca Moorish style
Moros y cristianos ('Moors & Christians') black beans with white rice
morragute thinlip grey mullet (fish)
morros cheeks
    morros de ternera beef cheeks
~*Morros de ternera a la vizcaína* Basque style beef cheeks with sauce
morruda sheepshead bream (fish)
mortadela mortadella
Morteruelo mixed meat pâté (cold) or hash (hot)
moruno/moruna Moorish
Moscatel grape producing sweet white wines
Mostachones crispy pine nut biscuits (cookies)
mostaza mustard
Mousse de gofio Canarian **gofio** (see) cream dessert
Mozkor salda *Bsq* garlic soup

mújol* grey mullet   [*general term for all species of this fish]
~*Mújol a la sal* grey mullet baked in salt
~*Mújol al horno con patatas* baked grey mullet with potatoes

~*Mújol cocido* grey mullet stew
mullador Valencian ratatouille
Murcia (Murcia al vino), queso de Murcian pasteurized goat's milk cheese
murciano/murciana Murcian style
musclo *Ctn* mussel
muslitos de cangrejo crab claws
muslo thigh
musola smooth hound (fish)

A Dictionary of Food in Spain

N

nabo turnip
    nabo sueco ('Swedish turnip') swede
nácar fan mussel
nacre *Ctn* fan mussel
ñame yam
Napolitanas de chocolate flaky pastries with chocolate
naranja orange
naranjada orangeade
nata cream
    Nata de Cantabria, queso Cantabrian semi-cured raw cow's milk cheese
    nata montada whipped cream
    nata para cocinar cream for cooking
    nata para montar pouring cream for desserts
natillas thin custard dessert made from milk, sugar, eggs, vanilla & cinnamon
navaja razor clam
navarro/navarra[1] Navarra style
Navarra[2] wine region (see map, p.117)

nécora velvet swimming crab
nectarina nectarine
Negramoll Canarian red wine grape
negro/negra black
Neula (*plural Neules*) Catalan thin rolled cylindrical biscuit (cookie) resembling the British 'brandy snap'

níscalo saffron milk cap (wild mushroom)
níspero loquat

nogal walnut
ñora mild sweet red pepper, usually dried

nuez (*plural* **nueces**) 1. walnut (usually) 2. nut (**fruto seco** is the usual term for this)
   nuez moscada nutmeg

O

o or

oblada saddled bream (fish)

oca goose
~*Oca asada* roast goose

ojiverde shortnose greeneye (fish)

oli *Ctn* oil
Oliaigua Menorcan style cold vegetable soup
    with garlic, onions, tomatoes & green peppers
~*Oliaigua de Menorca* = *Oliaigua* (above)
olla pot
~*Olla cordobesa* Cordoban style vegetable stew
~*Olla podrida* Burgos style assorted meats, vegetables & bean
    or chickpea stew
Ollada Valencian meat & vegetable stew
oloroso dry, dark & nutty sherry

orada *Ctn* gilt-head bream (fish)
orégano oregano
oreja ear
    oreja de mar abalone (marine snail)
orejón dried apricot
orella *Ctn* ear
    orella de mar abalone (marine snail)
Orelletes *Ctn* thin fried Catalan festive sugar-coated pastries
orenyola *Ctn* flying fish
oriola vera *Ctn* grey gurnard (fish)
orujo = aguardiente de orujo
orxata *Ctn* = **horchata**

osobuco cross-cut beef or veal shank
ostión Portuguese oyster

~***Ostiones a la gaditana*** Cádiz style oven-baked oysters with garlic, parsley, olive oil & breadcrumbs
ostra oyster
~***Ostras fritas*** fried oysters with egg & cornmeal coating

ou de mar *Ctn* grooved sea squirt

oveja 1. sheep 2. ewe

P

Pa amb tomàquet *Ctn* Catalan toasted bread rubbed with tomatoes, sprinkled with salt, & drizzled withn olive oil
pacana pecan
pada *Ctn* horn-shell (single-shell mollusc)
Paella *Ctn* 1. a traditional short grain rice dish of Valencian origin, cooked in a flat pan together with saffron, vegetables, meats & seafood, often mixed; the composition is highly variable 2. pan, especially for cooking paella (see illustration on Title Page)
~***Paella catalana*** paella with chicken, **longaniza** (see), crayfish, prunes & peas or artichokes
~***Paella de fideos*** = ***Cazuela de fideos***
~***Paella de marisco*** paella with seafood
~***Paella de pollo*** paella with chicken
~***Paella marinera*** = ***Paella de marisco*** (above)
~***Paella mixta*** mixed paella with pork, chicken & seafood
~***Paella parellada*** Barcelona style mixed paella with completely peeled shellfish & boneless meats
~***Paella valenciana*** paella with chicken & rabbit
paellera flat pan for cooking ***Paella*** (above)
pagell *Ctn* pandora (fish)
pagre *Ctn* sea bream (fish)
pagro sea bream (fish)
pàguera *Ctn* sea bream (fish)
pajarito small bird
palaia *Ctn* flatfish
    palaia bruixa *Ctn* 1. megrim 2. four-spot megrim
    palaia misèries *Ctn* Mediterranean scaldfish
    palaia petit *Ctn* 1. French sole 2. Klein's sole
    palaia rossa *Ctn* 1. spotted flounder 2. Thor's scaldfish
paleta[1] 1. lamb shoulder 2. pork hand
    paleta ibérica dried shoulder ham
Paleta[2] ice lolly
paletilla shoulder (animal)

Palmero, queso Canarian smoked & unsmoked semi-hard raw goat's milk cheese
palmito 1. heart of palm 2. palmetto
paloma 1. squab 2. pigeon 3. dove
palometa pompano (fish)
    palometa blanca pompano (fish)
    palometa negra 1. pomfret (fish) 2. Atlantic pomfret 3. Ray's bream (fish)
~Palometa frita fried pompano (or pomfret. etc.)
palometón leerfish
palomida *Ctn* leerfish
Palomino white grape used mainly to produce dry sherry
pámpano pomfret (fish)
pamplona Pamplona style
pàmpol *Ctn* pilot fish
pan bread
    pan cateto rustic bread
    pan cortado sliced bread
    pan de centeno rye bread
    pan de leche soft milk bread
    pan de molde ('moulded bread') regular loaf of bread
    pan integral wholemeal bread
    pan rallado breadcrumbs
    pan sin corteza bread without crusts
~Pan con tomate y jamón Catalan style bread with tomato & ham
~Pan de bizcocho sponge cake
~Pan de higo fig roll
panadería bakery
panadera baker (female)
panadero baker (male)
Panades Balearic lamb & pea pasties
Panadons amb espinacs *Ctn* Catalan spinach pasties
panceta 1. fatty pork 2. streaky bacon 3. pancetta
    panceta de cerdo belly pork
panecillo 1. bread roll 2. roll (bun) 3. bap
panegall *Ctn* blue-mouth (fish)
Panellets *Ctn* Catalan almond & potato biscuits (cokies) for All Saints' Day

panga cheap fish
papas potatoes
~*Papas arrugadas* = *Patatas arrugadas*
para for
    Para picar nibbles
pardete grey mullet (fish)
Parellada Catalan still white wine grape
pargo sea bream (fish)
~*Pargo encebollado* sea bream in onion sauce
parrilla grill (broiler)
    a la **parrilla** grilled (broiled)
Parrillada 1. barbecued or grilled (broiled) dish 2. mixed grill
~*Parrillada de patatas* barbecued potatoes
parrocha sardine
pasa[1] raisin
paso/pasa[2] dried (fruit)
pasta 1. pasta 2. pastry 3. paste 4. purée 5. biscuit (cookie)
    pasta quebrada flaky pastry
~*Pastas castañuelas* Valladolid castonet-shaped fig pastries with chocolate coating
pastel 1. pie 2. pastry 3. pasty (hand pie)
~*Pastel a la murciana* Murcian style chicken pie
~*Pastel de berenjenas* baked aubergine (eggplant) mousse
~*Pastel de carne* meat pie
~*Pasteles de gloria* little pastries filled with sweet potato & ground almonds
~*Pasteles de almendras* fried almond pasties
Pastelillo 1. turnover 2. pasty (hand pie)
~*Pastelillos de pescado* semicircular fish pasties
Pastelito little pie
~*Pastelitos de carne* little meat pies
pastenaga *Ctn* female cuckoo wrasse (fish)
Pastissets *Ctn* Catalan crecent-shaped sweet stuffed fried pastries (sweet potato or sweet almond filling)
pastor shepherd
pastora shepherdess
pata leg (animal)
Pataco Catalan style tuna casserole with snails

patata potato
~*Patatas a la cerdeña* Sardinian style potatoes with garlic
   & bacon
~*Patatas a la importancia* Castilian-Leonese battered
   potatoes, fried & then cooked in garlic & saffron mash
~*Patatas a la panadera* Baker's potato caserole with onions
~*Patatas a la riojana* Rioja style potatoes with pork
~*Patatas a lo pobre* Poor man's fried potatoes with onions,
   salt & olive oil; other versions include bell peppers or are
   coated in garlic mayonnaise; sometimes with fried egg
~*Patatas al ajo cabañil* Murcian 'muleteer's' garlic potatoes
~*Patatas alioli* fried potatoes in garlic mayonnaise
~*Patatas arrugadas* Canarian style small whole potatoes
   boiled until wrinkled, lightly roasted & served
   with **mojo** (see) sauce
~*Patatas bravas* spicy potato chunks
~*Patatas con mejillones* potatoes with mussels
~*Patatas en salsa verde* potatoes in green sauce
~*Patatas fritas* 1. chips (French fries) 2. crisps (chips) in a bag
~*Patatas meneás* = *Patatas revolconas* (below)
~*Patatas revolconas* mashed potato with paprika & bacon
~*Patatas viudas* 'widowed' (meatless) potatoes with onion,
   garlic & herbs
pato duck
~*Pato a la sevillana* Sevillian style duck with olives & orange
Patxaran *Bsq* sloe liqueur
pavo turkey
~*Pavo adobado* pot roast of marinated turkey
~*Pavo asado a la catalana* Catalan style roast turkey
~*Pavo en adobo* = *Pavo adobado* (above)
~*Pavo en escabeche a la extremeña* Extremaduran style
   marinated cooked turkey
~*Pavo trufado* truffled boned turkey
Payoyo, queso Grazalema (Cádiz) ewe's & goat's milk cheese

pebre pepper
pechuga breast (of poultry)
   pechugo de pollo chicken breast
   pechugo de pollo filetada sliced chicken breast

pechugo de pollo entera whole chicken breast
~Pechuga de pollo a la sevillana Sevillian style chicken breast with olives
pedaç *Ctn* wide-eyed flounder (fish)
Pedro Ximénez 1. sweet sherry 2. the grape used
peix (*plural* **peixos**) *Ctn* fish (any)
    peix de San Rafel *Ctn* red gurnard
    peix espada *Ctn* swordfish
    peix rei *Ctn* 1. whiting 2. blue whiting
~Peix al forn *Ctn* baked fish
~Peix al forn a la mallorquina Mallorcan style baked fish with potatoes & spinach or Swiss chard
~Peix en es forn *Ctn* = *Peix al forn* (above)
peixator *Ctn* fishmonger
peixe (*plural* **peixes**) *Gal* fish (any)
pejerrey big-scale sand smelt (fish)
Peladillas sugar-coated almonds
pelado/pelada peeled
Pella de gofio Canarian milk & **gofio** (see) dessert patty
Pelota large pork meatball, often served in cabbage leaf or lettuce wrap
peluda 1. scaldback (fish) 2. Mediterranean scaldfish 3. Imperial scaldfish 4. Thor's scaldfish 5. whiskered sole (fish)
Peñamellera Asturian cow's milk cheese, with goat's or ewe's milk added in spring & summer for added flavour
Penedès wine region of N.E. Spain (see map, p.117)
pepinillo cucumber pickle
pepino cucumber
pepitoria 1. fricassee 2. egg yolk & almond sauce
    en **pepitoria** in egg yolk & almond sauce
~Pepitoria de pollo chicken fricassee
pera pear
~Peras al horno oven-baked pears
~Peres de Lleida *Ctn* Catalan peeled pears cooked in light custard & served cold with meringue & cherries
perca perch (fish)
percebes goose barnacles
perdiu *Ctn* 1. partridge 2. see *Arroz en perdiu*

perdiz (*plural* **perdices**) partridge
~Perdices a la casera home style partridge casserole
~Perdices a la mesonera hostess style roasted partridges with ham, vegetables, fresh tomato sauce, wine & sherry
~Perdices a la navarra Navarra style partridge casserole
~Perdices a lo torero bullfighter style giblet-stuffed partridge casserole with anchovies, bacon & bell peppers
~Perdices en escabeche (Perdices escabechadas) pickled partridges
~Perdiz en chocolate stewed partridge with grated chocolate
~Perdiz estofado partridge stew
peregrina scallop (bivalve mollusc)
perejil parsley
perifollo chervil
perlon 1. grey gurnard (fish) 2. tub gurnard
Perolada Valencian meat & vegetable stew
pescadilla small hake (fish)
~Pescadilla a la parrilla grilled (broiled) small hake
pescado fish (any)
~Pescado al horno oven-baked fish (e.g. sea bream)
~Pescado blanco en ajillo white fish with garlic
~Pescado blanco a la malagueña Málaga style boiled white fish with sauce
~Pescado en escabeche marinated fish
~Pescado frito deep-fried floured fish
~Pescado seco Canarian dried fish dish; may include roasted **jareas** (see) & *Tollos* (see)
Pescaíto frito = *Pescado frito* (above)
pescuezo 1. lamb neck 2. beef neck
Pestiños sweet flour dough fritters
pesto pesto sauce
Pets de monja *Ctn* Catalan 'nun's' nipple-like biscuits
petxina de pelegri *Ctn* pilgrim scallop (bivalve mollusc)
petxinot *Ctn* dog-cockle (bivalve mollusc)
peu de cabrit Noah's ark (bivalve mollusc)
pez (*plural* **peces**) fish (any)
    pez aguja Atlantic white marlin
    pez angel angel-fish
    pez ballesta trigger-fish

pez cinto scabbard fish
pez de limón amberjack
pez de San Francisco lizard fish
Pez de San Pedro John dory
pez espada swordfish
pez martillo hammerhead
pez piloto pilot fish
pez plata argentine
pez volador flying fish
~*Pez espada a la malagueña* Málaga style swordfish casserole
~*Pex espada en amarillo* swordfish in saffron sauce
~*Pez de limón al hinojo* charcoal-grilled (broiled) amberjack with fennel

Picada[1] 1. appetizer 2. snack 3. nibbles
    picada catalana Catalan crushed nut & parley sauce
picadillo 1. mince (noun) 2. chopped vegetables or meat
~*Picadillos almerienses* Almería style chopped beef & pork
~*Picadilla de patatas* hash browns
picado/picada[2] 1. minced (ground) 2. chopped
picante 1. spicy 2. piquant 3. hot
pichón 1. squab 2. pigeon 3. dove
~*Pichones estofados* stew of young pigeons
Picón Bejes-Tresviso Cantabrian blue cheese made from a blend of cow's, ewe's & goat's milk
picota cherry
pierna leg
    pierna de cordero leg of lamb
~*Pierna de cordero asado* roast leg of lamb
~*Pierna de cordero guisado con judías blancas* Casseroled leg of lamb with white beans
Pijama elaborate dessert of **flan** (see) with ice creams, canned fruit & cream
pijota hake (fish)
pil-pil sauce of Basque origin made from oil in which fish has been cooked with garlic & chili peppers
    al **pil-pil** with pil-pil sauce
pimentón paprika
    pimentón dulce sweet paprika

pimentón dulce ahumado smoked sweet paprika
pimentón picante hot paprika
pimentón picante ahumado smoked hot paprika
pimienta pepper (spice)
    pimienta en grano peppercorns
    pimienta negra black pepper
pimiento pepper (vegetable)
    pimiento rojo red bell pepper
    pimiento verde green bell pepper
~*Pimientos a la malagueña* Málaga style bell peppers with onion & raisins
~*Pimientos de Padrón* fried small green Padrón peppers (some unpredictably hot) served as a *Tapa* (see)
~*Pimientos fritos* fried bell peppers
~*Pimientos rellenos* stuffed bell peppers
piña pineapple
    piña de millo corn on the cob (Canarian)
Pinchitos charcoal-grilled (broiled) small pieces of matrinated pork on wooden skewers
Pincho 1. N. Spain bar snack, ingredients often spiked to a piece of bread with a stick ('Basque tapa on a stick'; see *Tapa*) 2. pointed stick used as a skewer
~*Pinchos de encurtidos = Banderillas*
~*Pinchos morunos = Pinchitos*
piñón pine nut
pintada Guinea fowl
pintarroja lesser-spotted dogfish
Pintxo Bsq = Pincho
Piparras = Banderillas
Piperrada Basque roasted bell pepper stew, sometimes with eggs
pipirrana fresh tomato relish
piquillo type of chili
Piriñaca Cádiz style tomato salad
pistacho pistachio
Pisto stewed summer vegetables (type of ratatouille)
pitu chicken (Asturian dialect)
    pitu caleya free-range chicken (Asturian dialect)
~*Pitu (de) caleya (con arroz)* Asturian style chicken & rice

plancha flat metal cooking plate (griddle)
  a la **plancha** griddled
plátano banana
platija flounder (fish)
plato 1. dish 2. plate
  primer **plato** starter
  segundo **plato** main course
~*Plato combinado* main & side on one plate, often including meat, fries & salad
~*Plato de carne a la parrilla* mixed grill
~*Plato especial* house special
plegonero whiting (fish)

pobre poor man's style
pochas freshly-shelled beans prior to drying
~*Pochas a la riojana* La Rioja style casserole of beans with small pieces of lambs' tails or lamb riblets
poco 1. a little 2. not much
  poco hecho cooked rare (steak)
podás wide-eyed flounder (fish)
polbo *Gal* octopus
~*Polbo á feira* *Gal* Galician 'fair style' octopus, potatoes & paprika, cooked in a special copper cauldron to give a unique flavour
pollo chicken
  pollo entero whole chicken
  pollo entero limpio gutted chicken without head or feet
  pollo troceado chopped-up chicken
~*Pollo a la cacerola española* Spanish chicken casserole
~*Pollo a la levantina* Levantine chicken with green peppers
~*Pollo a la manchega* La Mancha style young chicken casserole with olives & vegetables
~*Pollo al ajillo* chicken with garlic
~*Pollo al chilindrón* chicken with bell peppers
~*Pollo al jerez* chicken with sherry
~*Pollo al vino* chicken braised in wine
~*Pollo asado* roast chicken
~*Pollo con tomate* chicken with tomato
~*Pollo en pepitoria* chicken fricassee with almonds

~*Pollo en salsa de vino* chicken in wine sauce
~*Pollo en samfaina a la catalana* Catalan style chicken with mixed vegetables (ratatouille)
~*Pollo granadina* Granada style chicken with ham
~*Pollo relleno* meat-stuffed chicken
Polvorón type of shortbread with almonds & cinnamon
pomelo grapefruit
~*Pomelos en almibar* grapefruit in syrup
ponche Spanish hot toddy with brandy
pop *Ctn* common octopus
    pop blanc *Ctn* curled octopus
por by
    por encargo by special order
porcino pork products (in general)
Porra antequerana Antequera style thick tomato & dried bread soup, usually served cold, sometimes topped with tuna or ham; mostly presented as a *Tapa* (see)
Porrupatata Basque stewed leeks with lots of potato
Porrusalda Basque stewed leeks, sometimes with salt cod; elsewhere in Spain, beef or sausage may be added
Postre dessert
potaje 1. potage 2. thick soup
~*Potaje a la catalana* Catalan thick chickpea & sausage soup
~*Potaje de garbanzos con espinacas* chickpea & spinach potage
~*Potaje de garbanzos y acelga* chickpea & chard potage
~*Potaje de habas secas* thick dried broad bean soup
~*Potaje madrileño* Madrid style potage of chickpeas, spinach & salt cod
Pote gallego Galician rustic bean & meat soup

prensado/prensada compressed
preparado/preparada barbacao prepared for the barbecue
presa pork shoulder
primavera spring (season)
primer first
    primer plato starter
Principe Alberto Canarian chocolate cake dessert
Pringá Andalusian slowly stewed roast beef or roast pork with cured sausage (**chorizo**, **morcilla**; see) & lard or suet; it can

be served on a plate, eaten by grasping the meat with pieces of bread (***Pringando***), or as a ***Tapa*** (see), where the meat is enclosed in bread rolls as a small sandwich
Pringando see ***Pringá*** (above)
Priorat Catalan rich red wine region (see map, p.117)
probecho grooved sea squirt
propina tip

Puchero 1. boiled dinner (one-pot meal) 2. stock pot
*~**Puchero de gallina*** stewed boiling fowl
*~**Puchero de las tres abocas*** Valencian stew with lamb
*~**Puchero canario*** Canarian style meat-rich soup & vegetables
pudenta *Ctn* pomfret
Pudín = ***Budín***
puerco pig
puerro leek
Pulpetas veal & ham roll-ups
pulpo common octopus
    pulpo blanco curled octopus
    pulpo patudo Atlantic white spotted octopus
*~**Pulpo a la gallega*** = ***Polbo á feira***
*~**Pulpos con papas*** octopus & potatoes
pulpón Atlantic white spotted octopus
Puntillitas fried battered little cuttlefish ***Tapa*** (see)
punys d'ous *Ctn* Menorcan hot egg punch
puput *Ctn* wide-eyed flounder (fish)
puré 1. purée 2. thick soup 3. paste
*~**Puré de habas*** broad bean purée
*~**Puré de San Juan*** thick kidney bean soup
*~**Puré de Vigilia*** thick Lenten soup of vegetables & salt cod
Purrusalda = ***Porrusalda***
Putxero *Ctn* = ***Puchero***

A Dictionary of Food in Spain

Q

queimada Galician alcoholic punch
queixo *Gal* cheese
quelet *Ctn* red bream (fish)
Quesadilla herreña Canarian cheese cake
Quesillo canario Canarian style dessert custard
queso cheese (see also by individual names)
    queso curado cheese aged for more than 3 months
    queso de cabra goat's milk cheese
    queso de oveja sheep's milk cheese
    queso duro hard cheese
    queso en polvo grated cheese
    queso fresco very young cheese
    queso gratinado grated cheese
    queso rallado grated cheese
    queso semicurado cheese aged for less than 4 months
~***Queso con anchoas*** a ***Tapa*** (see) of cured cheese topped with anchovies
~***Queso frito*** fried breaded sliced cheese

quintería farmhouse style
quisquilla common prawn (shrimp)
    quisquilla gris brown shrimp
quissona *Ctn* spur dog (fish)

A Dictionary of Food in Spain

R

rábano radish
    rábano picante horseradish
Rabas crispy fried battered or breaded squid, cut into rings or strips or other shapes, & served as a ***Tapa*** (see)
rabo 1. tail 2. oxtail
    rabo de buey oxtail
    rabo de toro oxtail (from a bull)
~***Rabo de toro a la sevillana*** Sevillian style braised oxtail
raboa *Ctn* blenny (fish)
ración 1. portion 2. helping 3. serving 4. ration
    media **ración** half portion (of a dish)
raia *Gal* skate (fish)
rajada de taques *Ctn* brown ray (fish)
rallado/rallada grated
Rancho canario Canarian soup with chickpeas, potatoes, lard, meat & thick noodles
rap *Ctn* angler-fish
Rapaduras Canarian cane sugar sweets (candies)
rape angler-fish
~***Rape a la langosta*** cold poached angler-fish as fake lobster
~***Rape a la marinera*** sailor's style angler-fish with clams & prawns (shrimp)
~***Rape al horno*** baked angler-fish
~***Rape en cacerola*** angler-fish casserole
~***Rape en salsa de almendras*** angler-fish in almond sauce
rascacio black scorpionfish
raspallón annular bream (fish)
rata star-gazer (fish)
ratafia Catalan liqueur
raya 1. skate (fish) 2. ray (various species of this fish)
    raya blanca bottlenose skate
    raya bramante bottlenose skate
    raya de clavos thornback ray
    raya de espejos brown ray
~***Raya en pimenton*** skate in paprika sauce

~Raya a la gallega Galician style skate wings with potatoes
~Raya a la malagueña Málaga style baked ray with almonds

Rebojo Zamoran sponge cake
Rebozadas[1] = *Buñuelos*
rebozado/rebozada[2] 1. coated in batter 2. coated in egg & breadcrumbs (breaded)
rebeco chamois
redondo beef topside (round)
refresco 1. soft drink 2. fizzy drink (pop)
reig *Ctn* meagre (fish)
relleno[1]/rellena stuffed
relleno[2] stuffing
remojo soaking
Remojón Granada style salt cod, orange & olive salad
rémol brill (fish)
rèmol de riu *Ctn* flounder (fish)
remolacha beetroot
~Remolachas a la vinagreta beetroot vinaigrette
reo sea trout
repollitos de Bruselas Brussels sprouts
repollo cabbage
~Repollo a la valenciana Valencian style cabbage with garlic, olives & capers
requesón cottage cheese
res cattle
reserva aged wine
restaurante restaurant
  restaurante vegano vegan restaurant
  restaurante vegetariano vegetarian restaurant
Revoltillo de huevo con tomate scrambled eggs with tomato
revuelto[1]/revuelta scrambled
revuelto[2] scrambled eggs
~Revuelto de... scrambled eggs with...
~Revuelto de champiñones scrambled eggs with mushrooms

Ribera del Duero northern plateau red wine producing area
  Ribera red wine from that region (see map, p.117)

ribereño/ ribereña 1. riverside-dweller style 2. riverine 3. coastal
riñón kidney
    riñón de cerdo pig's kidney
    riñón de cordero lamb's kidney
~*Riñones al jerez* sautéed kidneys (any) with sherry
~*Riñones con champiñones* lamb's kidneys with mushrooms
rio river
Rioja 1. wine region of North-Central Spain (see map, p.117) 2. popular dry red wines from that region
riojano/riojana La Rioja style
Rizos de lenguado fried rolled sole fillets, secured with toothpicks

rodaballo turbot (fish)
rodaja slice
    rodajas de salmón salmon steaks cut crosswise
rojo/roja red
rollo roll
~*Rollo de carne* meat roll, served hot or cold
rombo brill (fish)
romero rosemary
romesco 1. dried sweet red pepper 2. = **salsa romesco**
rompope eggnog
Roncal raw ewe's milk cheese from Navarra
rondeño/rondeña Ronda style
Ropa vieja ('Old clothes') leftover beef cooked with chickpeas or vegetables & tomato sauce; in the Canaries it is a dish of shredded beef & chicken, with potatoes & chickpeas
rosada[1] common term for fillets of various dogfish
rosado/rosada[2] 1. pink 2. rosé (wine)
Rosbif roast beef, sliced at cold counter
Rosca 1. donut 2. bagel-like bread roll
Rosco 1. donut 2. bread roll
~*Roscos de huevo* egg donuts
~*Roscos fritos* fried donuts
Roscón de Reyes ring-shaped cake for Kings' Day
Rosquetes Canarian ring-shaped fried pastries

Rosquillas ring-shaped deep-fried donuts (many varieties)
*~**Rosquillas de vino*** Extremaduran white wine, olive oil & lemon donuts
Rossejat d'arròs = ***Arroz rossejat***
Rostit humit *Ctn* Balearic pot roast
roto/rota broken
rovellons *Ctn* wild bloody milk cap mushrooms
Rovellons a la brasa Catalan style charcoal-grilled (broiled) bloody milk cap mushrooms

rubio streaked gurnard (fish)
*~**Rubio a la naranja*** gurnard in orange sauce
rubiols Balearic semicircular pastries with various sweet or savoury fillings
Rueda Castilian-Leonese wine region (see map, p.117)
ruso/rusa Russian

S

sábalo thwaite shad (fish)
saboga thwaite shad (fish)
sabre *Ctn* scabbard fish
sal salt
    a la **sal** cooked in salt
    con **sal** salted
salchicha fresh pork sausage
salchichón cured sausage (salami)
salda *Bsq* soup
salema salema (fish)
salmón salmon
~*Salmón a la gallega* Galician style salmon poached in alcoholic broth
~*Salmón a la ribereña* Asturian 'river-dweller's style' salmon with ham in cider sauce
~*Salmón con aceitunas* salmon casserole with olives
salmonete red mullet (fish)
    salmonete de fango red mullet
    salmonete de roca surmullet
~*Salmonetes a la plancha con aliño* griddled red mullet with sauce
~*Salmonetes con salsa de anchoas* red mullet with anchovy sauce
~*Salmonetes con salsa romesco* grlled (broiled) red mullet with romesco sauce (see **salsa romesco**)
Salmorejo Andalusian thick tomato soup, served cold
salpa *Ctn* salema (fish)
Salpicón salad with chopped meat, fish or shellfish mixed with vinaigrette
~*Salpicón de mariscos* shellfish cocktail
salsa sauce
    salsa andaluza Andalusian pumpkin sauce
    salsa de aceitunas olive sauce
    salsa de almendras almond sauce

salsa de cabrales blue cheese sauce
salsa de piñones pine nut sauce
salsa de tomate tomato sauce
salsa gallega = ajada gallega
salsa mayonesa mayonnaise
salsa romesco Tarragona dried sweet red pepper sauce
salsa vinagreta vinaigrette
salteado/salteada sautéed
saludo/saluda 1. salted 2. salty
salvado bran
salvia sage
sama de pluma pink dentex (fish)
Samfaina *Ctn* Jewish-Muslim ratatouille
San Saint
    San Pedro John dory (fish)
    San Simón da Costa Galician smoked conical raw or pasteurized cow's milk cheese
Sancocho canario fish with Canarian red sauce
sandía watermelon
sangre blood
sangri menorqui *Ctn* Menorcan style mulled wine
sangria red wine & fruit punch
sard *Ctn* white sea bream (fish)
sardina 1. sardine 2. pilchard
~***Sardinas a la moruna*** Moorish style casserole of sardines with garlic, cumin, saffron & paprika
~***Sardinas rellenos*** stuffed sardines
sardinillas little sardines
sargo white sea bream (fish)
sarmiento dried vine branch
    al **sarmiento** cooked over vine branch embers
Sarró de cabra pasteurized goat's milk cheese produced near Barcelona
sarten frying pan

sebo suet
seco/seca 1. dry 2. dried
secreto de cerdo special tasty cut of pork near the shoulder
segundo plato ('second plate') main course

sepia cuttlefish
~Sepia a la mallorquina Mallorcan style cuttlefish stew with raisins & pine nuts
sèpia *Ctn* cuttlefish
serrà *Ctn* comber (fish)
serrandell scaldfish
serranito containing serrano ham (see **jamón serrano**)
serrano[1] painted comber (fish)
serrano[2]/**serrana** mountain style
servicio service charge
    servicio incluido service charge (tip) included
    servicio no incluido service charge (tip) not included
servido/servida served
    servido con served with
servilleta serviette (napkin)
    Servilleta, queso fresco de Valencian young pasteurized goat's milk cheese
sesos brains
~Sesos huecos fried battered poached brains
seta 1. mushroom 2. porcini mushroom
~Setas al ajillo mushrooms sautéed in olive oil & garlic
~Setas al jerez braised mushrooms with sherry
sevillano/sevillana Sevillian style

sidra cider
sin without
    sin colorantes artificiales without artificial colouring
    sin conservantes artificiales without artificial preservatives
    sin gluten without gluten
    sin leche without milk
sípia *Ctn* cuttlefish
sipió *Ctn* little cuttlefish

sobrasada Balearic raw cured pork sausage with paprika
socarrat crusty layer at bottom of paella pan
Socochones Extremaduran rich chestnut & milk dessert
sofrito fried tomato sauce
soja soy

soldat *Ctn* foureyed sole (fish)
Soldaditos de Pavía fried cod wrapped in slices of roasted red bell pepper, often served as a ***Tapa*** (see)
solla 1. European plaice (fish) 2. European flounder (fish) 3. common dab (fish)
solleta spotted flounder (fish)
solomillo 1. beef fillet steak (filet mignon) 2. pork fillet (tenderloin) 3. chicken breast mini-fillets
~***Solomillo a la castellana*** small fried pork or beef medallions served as a ***Tapa*** (see) with an onion or Cabrales cheese sauce
~***Solomillo al whisky*** small pork or beef medallions marinated in whisky, brandy or white wine & fried in olive oil; served as a ***Tapa*** (see)
~***Solomillo de cerdo al jerez*** pork fillet with sherry
sonso *Ctn* Mediterranean sand eel
Sopa soup
~***Sopa al cuarto de hora*** ('15 minute soup') shellfish soup
~***Sopa cachorreña*** Andalusian soup made with bitter oranges, garlic, paprika & bread; desalted salt cod may be added
~***Sopa con costrón*** soup with egg & cheese crust
~***Sopa de ajo*** garlic soup
~***Sopa de ajo a la Asmesnal*** garlic soup with cooked chicken & poached egg
~***Sopa de ajo blanco*** white garlic soup with ground almonds, & sometimes grapes or melon slices
~***Sopa de ajo blanco con uvas*** white garlic soup with grapes
~***Sopa de ajo con mayonesa*** garlic soup with mayonnaise
~***Sopa de albóndigas a la catalana*** Catalan meatball soup
~***Sopa de almendras*** almond soup
~***Sopa de Aragón*** Aragonese soup with beef liver & cheese
~***Sopa de cangrejos de rio*** crayfish soup
~***Sopa de chícharos*** Valladolid pea soup
~***Sopa de col mallorquina*** Mallorcan cabbage soup
~***Sopa de coles a la asturiana*** Asturian cabbage soup with sliced *chorizo* sausage & grated cheese
~***Sopa de gato*** ('Cat soup') Cádiz style garlic soup with grated cheese (*no* cat meat here!)
~***Sopa de guisantes*** = ***Sopa de chícharos*** (above)

~*Sopa de mejillones* mussel soup
~*Sopa de ostras* oyster soup
~*Sopa de pan con gambas* Andalusian bread soup with prawns (shrimp)
~*Sopa de pescado* fish soup
~*Sopa de pescado con mayonesa* Andalusian fish soup with mayonnaise
~*Sopa de picadillo* soup made from the broth of leftover stew
~*Sopa de rape* angler-fish soup
~*Sopa granadina* Granada vegetable soup with roasted garlic
~*Sopa leonesa* Leonese soup with milk, semolina, cinnamon, beef dripping & lemon zest
~*Sopa viña AB* fish soup with sherry
~*Sopa y bullit mallorquín* Mallorcan meat & vegetable soup
~*Sopas de ajo* garlic soup
~*Sopas mallorquinas* hearty Mallorcan vegetable soup, sometimes with added meat or sausage
Soplillos granadinos Granada style almond neringue puffs
Sorbete sorbet
~*Sorbete de fruta* fruit sorbet
sorell *Ctn* horse mackerel (fish)
Sorropotún = Marmitako
sortija French sole (fish)

sueco/sueca Swedish style
suela Klein's sole (fish)
Suizos sweet rolls
supermercado supermarket
Suquet de peix *Ctn* Catalan fish stew
Suquillo del pescador fisherman's seafood stew
surenys *Ctn* porcini mushroom
surtido[1] assortment
    surtido de postres assorted desserts (*literally* 'assortment of desserts')
surtido[2]**/surtida** assorted

A Dictionary of Food in Spain

T

tabla board
    tabla de quesos cheeseboard
talau (talo) Basque maize-flour flatbread eaten alone, with toppings or as a wrap
tallaetes *Ctn* slices
tambor real foureyed sole (fish)
Tapa (*plural Tapas*) bar snack; can be any dish, hot or cold, served in small portions
~*Tapas variadas* plate of various selected tapas
tapilla beef topside (round)
tarraconense Tarragon style
Tarta 1. cake 2. tart
~*Tarta de carne* meat pie
~*Tarta dev manzana* apple tart
~*Tarta de Santiago* almond pie dessert
~*Tarta helada* frozen torte (cake)
tasarte plain bonito (fish)
tasca tavern, serving *Tapas* (see)

té tea
    té verde green tea
Teja dumpling-shaped confection with druit or nuts
templado/templada 1. lukewarm 2. at room temperature (wine)
Tempranillo black grape yielding full-bodied red wines
tenca tench (fish)
~*Tencas en escabeche* fried or poached marinated tench
tenedor fork
tercio 33ml bottle of beer
ternera 1. beef 2. veal
    ternera en lata corned beef
    ternera para asar beef joint for roasting
    ternera para freír beef frying steak
    ternera para guisar stewing beef
    ternera picada minced (ground) beef

~*Ternera asada* roast veal
~*Ternera mechada* larded veal pot roast
Tetilla, queso Galician pear-shaped cow's milk cheese

de **tiempo** at room temperature (wine)
tienda shop
tierno/tierna 1. unripe 2. tender
tigres stuffed mussels
tila 1. lime blossom 2. lime blossom tea
tinta 1. ink 2. squid ink 3. cuttlefish ink
tinto red wine
    tinto de Verona mixture of red wine & a carbonated drink
tintorera blue shark

tocino 1. bacon 2. pork fat 3. lard
~*Tocino de cielo* ('Bacon from heaven') caramel-topped custard dessert, resembling a slab of bacon
Tollos Canarian dish of desalted sun-dried tope (shark), served with vegetables and sauce
tomate tomato
    tomate frito tomato, onion & garlic sauce
    tomates en rama tomatoes on the vine
    tomates triturados chopped tomatoes
~*Tomates rellenos* stuffed tomatoes
~*Tomates rellenos con ensaladilla rusa* tomatoes stuffed with Russian salad
~*Tomates rellenos de atún* tomatoes stuffed with tuna
Tombet = *Tumbet*
tomillo thyme
tonyina *Ctn* 1. tuna (tunny) 2. little tunny
~*Tonyina en escabetx* *Ctn* marinated tuna
tordo green wrasse (fish)
torero bullfighter style
torillo blenny (fish)
toro bull
toronja grapefruit
Torrezno fried bacon snack
Torrijas 'French toast', served as a dessert
Torró *Ctn* nougat

Torta round flat cake, bun or biscuit (cookie)
~*Torta cuajada* cheese cake
~**Torta de Casar** Extremaduran flat raw ewe's milk cheese
~**Torta de platano** banana cake
~*Tortas de aceite* flaky Sevillian biscuits (cookies)
~*Tortas de chicharrones* pork rind cakes
Tortell *Ctn* Catalan ring-shaped cake, usually stuffed with marzipan, but may be stuffed with jam, chocolate, etc.
Tortell de Reis = *Tortell* (above)
Tortilla omelette (omelet)
~*Tortilla capuchina* potato & asparagus omelette
~*Tortilla de chorizo* omelette with **chorizo** (see) sausage
~*Tortilla de espinacas* spinach omelette
~*Tortilla de gambas* prawn omelette (shrimp omelet)
~*Tortilla de patatas* = *Tortilla española* (below)
~*Tortilla de sardinas frescas* Balearic fresh sardine omelette
~*Tortilla de sesos* omelette with brains
~*Tortilla del Sacromonte* Granada omelette, usually with ham & kidneys; but authentically with lamb's brains & testes
~*Tortilla española* Spanish potato omelette
~*Tortilla murciana* Murcian style omelette with tomatoes, bell peppers & aubergine (eggplant)
~*Tortilla paisana* omelette with vegetables & **chorizo** (see)
Tortillita 1. fritter 2. small pancake
~*Tortillitas de camarones a la gaditana* Cádiz style fritters of tiny shrimp
~*Tortillitas de pasas* raisin pancakes
Tortita de Barros Extremaduran ewe's or goat's milk cheese
tórtola turtle dove
tostado/tostada toasted
Tostón roast suckling pig
~*Tostón asado* = *Tostón* (above)

Trempó *Ctn* Mallorcan summer salad
trigo wheat
tripotx lamb blood sausage
troceado/troceada chopped up
Tronchón Teruel raw or pasteurized ewe's & goat's milk cheese, sometimes with added cow's milk

trozito de... 1. a little slice of... 2. a little piece of...
trozo de... 1. a slice of... 2. a piece of...
trucha trout
~***Truchas a la asturiana*** Asturian style fried trout with bacon or salt pork
~***Truchas a la judía*** Jewish style baked trout with green sauce
~***Truchas a la navarra*** Navarra style fried trout stuffed with serrano ham
~***Truchas a la zamorana*** Zamora style poached trout
~***Trucha con unto*** grilled (broiled) trout stuffed with lard
trufa truffle
trufado/trufada truffled

Ttoro *Bsq* Basque fish & shellfish stew

tuétano bone marrow
Tumbet Mallorcan ratatouille
~***Tumbet de pecado mallorquin*** Mallorcan casserole of fish, tomatoes, bell peppers & aubergines (eggplants)
tupí[1] *Ctn* Catalan clay pot
Tupí[2] *Ctn* Catalan cow's, goat's or ewe's milk cheese mixed with liqueurs or olive oil, & fermented in a clay pot
Turrón 1. nougat 2. almond & honey candy bar

Txakoli *Bsq* Basque fruity dry white wine
Txangurro *Bsq* Basque spider crab casserole
txipirones *Bsq* = **chipirones**
txistorra *Bsq* = **chistorra**
txuleta (*plural* **txuletak**) *Bsq* chop
~***Txuletak parrilan*** *Bsq* grilled (broiled) chops

U ~ V

Ull de Llebre = Tempranillo

unto 1. animal fat 2. lard
    unto de puerco lard

urogallo capercaillie (wood grouse)
urta red-banded sea bream (fish)
~*Urta a la Roteña* Roteña (Cádiz) style braised or baked red-banded sea bream with bell peppers

uva grape
    uva pasa raisin

vaca 1. cow 2. *Ctn* painted comber (fish)
vacuno beef, mainly that which is minced (ground)
    vacuno/cerdo minced beef & pork mix
vairó *Ctn* pilot fish
Valdeón, queso de creamy blue cheese from the Picos de Europa Mountains, made from pure cow's milk or a blend of cow's, ewe's & goat's milk cheese
Valdepeñas central Spanish wine region (see map, p.117)
Valencia wine region (see map, p.117)
vapor steam
    al **vapor** steamed
variada[1] two-banded bream (fish)
variado/variada[2] various
vasco/vasca Basque style
vaso glass (for water)
    vaso de agua glass of tap water
    vaso de agua de grifo glass of tap water

vegano/vegana vegan (adjective & ♂/♀ person)
vegetal derived from plants
vegetariano/vegetariana vegetarian (adjective & ♂/♀ person)

venado venison
venta rural Andalusian roadside eatery, serving good quality inexpensive local dishes
verano summer
verat *Ctn* mackerel (fish)
verde green
Verdejo grape producing light-bodied white wines
verderol *Ctn* young amberjack (fish)
verduras 1. vegetables (in general) 2. greens

vibora starry weever (fish)
vieira scallop (bivalve mollusc)
~*Vieiras a la gallega* Galician style grilled (broiled) scallops with sauce & breadcrumbs
vinagre vinegar
vinagreta vinaigrette
vino wine
    vino blanco white wine
    vino de la casa house wine
    vino de tiempo wine at room temperature
    vino dulce sweet wine
    vino frío chilled wine
    vino joven young wine
    vino rancio well-matured (mellow) wine
    vino rosado rosé
    vino seco dry wine
    vino semiseco semi-dry (demi-sec) wine
    vino tinto red wine
viuda 1. widowed 2. meatless
vizcaíno/vizcaína Biscay style

volandeira type of scallop (bivalve mollusc)

X ~ Y ~ Z

xai *Ctn* lamb
xanquet *Ctn* Mediterranean sand smelt (fish)
Xareló grape for producing still & sparkling white wines
xató *Ctn* nut-based Catalan sauce for salad

xigala *Ctn* flat lobster
xiringuito *Ctn* beachside bar

xucla *Ctn* picarel (fish)
xuclador *Ctn* sea lamprey (fish)
xufa *Ctn* tiger nut
Xuixo *Ctn* deep-fried, sugar-coated, cylindrical pastry filled with custard

y and
yema 1. egg yolk 2. small cake based on egg-yolk pastry

zamboriña type of scallop (bivalve mollusc)
~*Zamboriñas* Galician scallops, often serves as a ***Tapa*** (see) in a tomato-based sauce
zamorano[1]/zamorana Zamora style
Zamorano[2], queso hard sheep's milk cheese from Zamora
zanahoria carot
zapata type of sea bream (fish)
Zarangolla Murcian scrambled eggs with courgettes (zucchini), onions & sometimes potatoes
Zarajo a Cuenca style ***Tapa*** (see) of fried or grilled (broiled) marinated suckling lamb's intestines rolled around two vine shoot sticks

Zarzuela Catalan style rich mixed seafood stew with almond paste & tomatoes
~***Zarzuela de mariscos*** = ***Zarzuela*** (above)
~***Zarzuela de pescado*** = ***Zarzuela*** (above)

zopa *Bsq* soup

zumo juice
    zumo de naranja exprimido freshly squeezed orange juice
zurracapote popular drink of red wine with fruit, sugar & cinnamon

Wine Regions of Mainland Spain
including lesser-known regions not mentioned in the Dictionary

A Dictionary of Food in Spain

© Colin B. Lessell

SOME USEFUL
WORDS & PHRASES

Politeness : POR FAVOR Please   GRACIAS Thank you

Food shopping

ABIERTO Store open   CERRADO Store closed

ESTOY BUSCANDO…   I'm lookimg for…

QUISIERA…   I'd like…

QUISIERA UN KILO DE…   I'd like a Kilo of…

QUISIERA DOSCIENTOS GRAMOS DE…   I'd like 200 grams of….

[Numbers: 1 uno 2 dos 3 tres 4 cuatro 5 cinco 6 seis 7 siete 8 ocho 9 nueve 10 diez 20 veinte 50 cincuenta 100 cien]

HAY… ?   Is/Are there any… ?
(pronounced like *eye* in English)

SI Yes   NO No

ACEPTAN TARJETAS DE CRÉDITO [O DÉBITO]?
Do you take credit [or debit] cards?

CUÁNTO CUESTA? How much is this? (enquiry before purchase)

CUÁNTO VA SER? How much will it be? (total at checkout)

NO NECESITO BOLSA   I don't need a bag

SIN GLUTEN   Without gluten

SIN LECHE Without milk

SIN COLORANTES ARTIFICIALES Without artificial colourants

SIN CONSERVANTES ARTIFICIALES Without artificial preservatives

CONSUMIR PREFERENTEMENTE ANTES DEL… Best before…

CONTIENE FRUTOS SECOS Contains nuts

Eating & drinking out

In a restaurant when you want the full menu, ask for LA CARTA (POR FAVOR). If you ask for EL MENÚ (POR FAVOR), you may be informed, in some establishments, of only the dishes of the day (i.e. MENÚ DEL DÍA). These are good value meals generally only served at lunchtime. They usually consist of three or four choices of a starter (PRIMER PLATO), several choices of a main course (SEGUNDO PLATO), wine (VINO), bread (PAN) & either a dessert (POSTRE) or coffee (CAFÉ).

If you wish to order **water**, but are on an economy drive, don't ask simply for AGUA. You will almost certainly be brought **bottled water** for which you must pay. Instead, order UN VASO DE AGUA (a glass of water), or more emphatically UN VASO DE AGUA DE GRIFO, in order to get **tap water**! Don't forget the POR FAVOR! In this regard, note that there are two words for **glass**: VASO usually means a glass for **water**, whereas COPA usually means one for **wine**. For two of you, order DOS VASOS DE AGUA [DE GRIFO].

When you want to order something, use (you know this from before) :
    QUISIERA... POR FAVOR   I'd like... please

Except in posher restaurants, the available red **wine** is mostly a RIOJA or a RIBERA. The available dry white is often an ALBARIÑO (grape) or a RUEDA (wine region).

    UNA BOTELLA DE VINO TINTO DE LA CASA
      A bottle of house red

    UNA MEDIA BOTELLA DE RIOJA A half-bottle of Rioja

    DOS COPAS DE ALBARIÑO Two glasses of Albariño

In the summer, red wine is often **chilled**; but if you want it at **room temperature**, order it DE TIEMPO.

A small draught (draft) **beer** in a glass (about 200ml) is a CAÑA. Otherwise, order CERVEZA according to brand & size.

Extra **cutlery** (CUBIERTOS) :

    CUCHILLO Knife   TENEDOR Fork   CUCHARA Spoon

When ordering a **steak**, there may be a choice :

ENTRECOT sirloin steak
LOMO ALTA ribeye steak
SOLOMILLO [DE TERNERA] fillet steak (filet mignon)
CHULETÓN a giant steak on the bone

You should say how you want it cooked. The choices are :

    POCO HECHO rare
    EN SU PUNTO medium-rare (recommended)
    MUY HECHO (or BIEN HECHO) well-done

Any dish, hot or cold, served in a very small portion, is a **TAPA**, unless it comes speared to a small piece of bread with a toothpick, when it becomes a Basque **PINTXO (PINCHO)**. A full portion of a dish is UNA **RACIÓN**, & a half portion is UNA **MEDIA RACIÓN**.

For those who decry meat, it may be best to search for a **vegetarian** or **vegan** restaurant (restaurante vegetariano/vegano), rather than struggle to discover whether they can truly go along with

    NO COMO CARNE, NI PESCADO I eat neither meat nor fish

As for having **allergies**, you could say, for example,

    TENGO ALERGIA A CACAHUETES! I'm allergic to peanuts!

    CONTIENE [TRAZOS DE] ALGÚN FRUTO SECO?
    Does it contain [traces of] any nuts?

And for getting **the bill (the check)**

    LA CUENTA POR FAVOR

As for a **tip** (PROPINA), it depends on the bill having

    SERVICIO INCLUIDO Service included
    SERVICIO NO INCLUIDO Service not included

And if you want to conserve your cash, remember

    ACEPTAN TARJETAS DE CRÉDITO [O DÉBITO]?

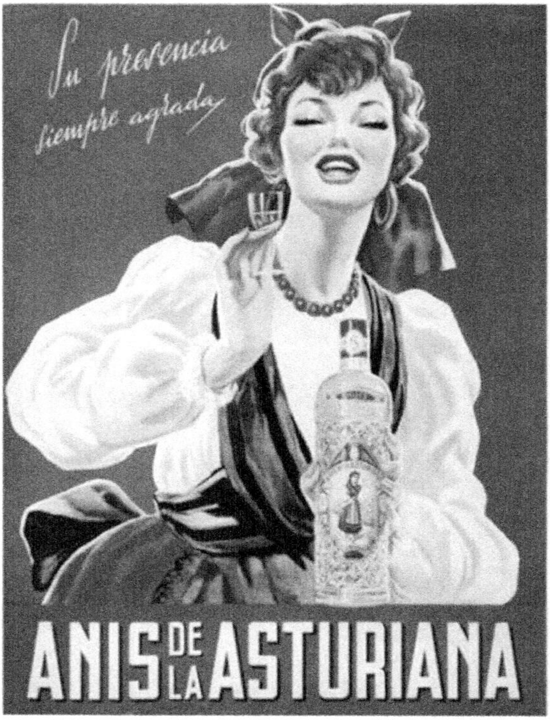
Su presencia
siempre agrada
ANIS DE LA ASTURIANA